The
Professionals' Guide
to
Fund Raising,
Corporate Giving,
and
Philanthropy

Recent Titles from Quorum Books

The
Professionals' Guide
to
Fund Raising,
Corporate Giving,
and
Philanthropy

PEOPLE GIVE TO PEOPLE

Lynda Lee Adams-Chau

Quorum Books

NEW YORK · WESTPORT, CONNECTICUT · LONDON

Library of Congress Cataloging-in-Publication Data

Adams-Chau, Lynda Lee.
    The professionals' guide to fund raising, corporate giving, and
philanthropy : people give to people / Lynda Lee Adams-Chau.
        p.   cm.
    Bibliography: p.
    Includes index.
    ISBN 0–89930–251–3 (lib. bdg. : alk. paper)
    1. Fund raising—United States.   I. Title.
HV41.9.U5A33   1988
361.7'068—dc19   87–32263

British Library Cataloguing in Publication Data is available.

Library of Congress Catalog Card Number: 87–32263
ISBN: 0–89930–251–3

First published in 1988 by Quorum Books

Greenwood Press, Inc.
88 Post Road West, Westport, Connecticut   06881

Printed in the United States of America

The paper used in this book complies with the Permanent Paper Standard issued
by the National Information Standards Organization (Z39.48–1984).

10 9 8 7 6 5 4 3 2 1

Contents

Preface

Philanthropy and volunteerism flourish in free societies. Under repressive governments they are stifled or destroyed. The Cultural Revolution in China repressed pluralism and diversity. My husband was a teenager in Guangzhou during that time. His father was a history and art teacher. The Red Guards' hostility was first directed at my father-in-law. They shaved his head, forced him to wear a dunce hat, and ridiculed him in front of an assembly of students that included his only son, my husband.

They also subjectd my husband to late-night interrogations and finally sent him to live for six years on a farm. Like so many others of China's "lost generation," he was forced to leave home to do manual labor. Yet, he and another man on the work production team organized their own private art club. My husband left China near the end of the Cultural Revolution. He is now a U.S. citizen, free to enjoy philanthropy and volunteerism in this country.

Although the cynic may charge that philanthropy and volunteerism perpetuate the chasm between the rich and the poor, the optimist will reply that they are the bridge across that chasm. Moreover, philanthropy is built upon a structure of tax laws. Thus, philanthropy is symbolic of U.S. democracy, far different from

China's totalitarianism. Each U.S. voter is free to elect representatives who will work to maintain the option of participation in philanthropy in this country.

Acknowledgments

I have enjoyed teaching "Successful Fund Raising" at Oral Roberts University for several years. I am grateful to the students who have taken the course, and I'm grateful for the opportunity to teach it and for my sabbatical year to complete this book. I also greatly appreciate Elaine Drain in ORU's Word Processing Center for typing the manuscript. Juliette Beaudry greatly assisted in proofreading. I list most of the guest speakers for my course in the chapters, and I am grateful for all of their participation. Others from foundations and corporations have helped me through correspondence. My family also gave me wonderful support for this project.

1

The Third Sector

INTRODUCTION

For the nation's first National Philanthropy Day, November 15, 1986, President Ronald Reagan said, "Philanthropy, as you know, is defined as an affection for mankind. Well, I think this benevolence flows from human freedom. It's when people are helping one another, not because they are taxed or coerced into it, but because they want to, that concern for one's fellow man becomes part of a nation's soul" (Reagan 1986:2). Nonprofit voluntary organizations seek funding from individuals, corporations, foundations, the United Way and other federated campaigns, churches and other religious organizations. Nonprofit voluntary organizations are also known as the "third sector" or "independent sector." The IRS may give them 501(c)(3) status.

Various national organizations help stimulate philanthropy and assure professionalism among both donors and recipients of funding. The Independent Sector is one such organization. Another is the National Committee for Responsive Philanthropy. Women and Foundations/Corporate Philanthropy is a national organization that concentrates on one gender. The National Society of Fund Raising Executives also serves to enhance professionalism among fund raisers. The American Association of Fund-Raising Counsel, Inc., is a professional organization for fund raising consultants. Finally, the Support Center provides fund raising and other management guidance and suggestions to nonprofit voluntary organizations.

501(c)(3) ORGANIZATIONS

Ever since the Revenue Act of 1913, the first constitutional income tax, third sector organizations have enjoyed tax exemption. Organizations in the third sector must meet certain IRS requirements in order to be exempt from taxation. The basic IRS regulation is known as 501(c)(3). Many donors will not contribute to nonprofit organizations unless they are 501(c)(3) organizations because donations are tax deductible only for 501(c)(3) organizations. Since 1917, a tax deduction for such donations has been available.

The IRS code states that 501(c)(3) organizations are "organized and operated exclusively for one or more of the following purposes: charitable, religious, educational, scientific, literary, testing for public safety, fostering national or international amateur sports competition . . . or the prevention of cruelty to children or animals." More than one-third of the organization's income must come from the public. For example, if the total support for an organization in the last three years was $600,000, then it must have received at least $200,000 from such general public sources as the government, the United Way, and individual donors to meet the one-third support test.

IRS Publication 557 and Package 1023 gives guidelines for 501(c)(3) applications. New organizations may apply for an advance ruling by the IRS on whether they will be granted 501(c)(3) status based on their estimated budgets. There is an appeal procedure if they are denied 501(c)(3) status.

Organizations file IRS Form 5768, Election/Revocation of Election by an Eligible Section 501(c)(3) Organization to Make Expenditures to Influence Legislation, to tell the IRS about any lobbying they will do. The term *lobby* originated during the time when citizens had to wait in the lobby to talk to their elected officials, who were the only ones allowed on the floor of public meeting halls. The IRS uses the term *lobby* to mean any attempt to influence not only elected officials but also any government employee or official, as well as any attempt to sway the public to influence legislation, called "grass roots lobbying." The IRS expenditure limits established by the Tax Reform Act of 1976 for direct lobbying are the lesser of $1 million or 20% of the exempt purpose expenditures up to $500,000; $100,000 plus 15% of the excess of the exempt purpose expenditures between $500,000 and $1 million; $175,000 plus 10% of the excess of the exempt purpose expenditures between $1 million and $1.5 million; or $225,000 plus 5% of the exempt purpose expenditures over $1.5 million. The grass roots nontaxable amount is 25% of that year's lobbying nontaxable amount.

When the 1976 IRS law was enacted, most nonprofit organizations were pleased because it allowed them to spend more money on lobbying. However, in November 1986 the IRS proposed regulations for the law that caused great consternation among many nonprofits. The proposed regulations broadened the definition of grass roots lobbying to include any fund raising or advertising material that includes even one sentence of lobbying information or any material that reaches the public inadvertently such as through media coverage of nonprofit testimony to legislators. Also, expenses of background research could be included as lobbying expenses, as could material expressing no explicit view on legislation, such as a newsletter. In addition, the new regulations were to be effective retroactively to 1977.

A 25% excise tax will be imposed on expenditures greater than the IRS limits. Organizations will lose their 501(c)(3) status if their lobbying expenditures are more than 150% greater than the limitations. Form 5768 gives organizations a safe harbor regarding lobbying expenditures. Otherwise, an organization is subject to a more vague standard that "no substantial part" of its activities will be lobbying.

INDEPENDENT SECTOR

The Independent Sector, at 1828 L Street, N.W., Washington, DC 20036, 202-659-4007 is a national organization that encourages nonprofit or third sector activities. Its charter meeting was held on March 5, 1980. It is the successor to the Coalition of National Voluntary Organizations, which formed in 1976, and the

National Council on Philanthropy, formed in 1954. Its membership includes nonprofit organizations, corporations, and foundations that contribute to nonprofit organizations. The name *independent* sector was preferred to *nonprofit* sector because of the negatives in the latter term, and was preferred to *third* sector because of the ambiguity in that term. The term *independent* includes a sense of independence from excessive government control.

John Gardner is the founder of Independent Sector. His inspiration to found the organization came when he attended a meeting of the Stanford University Board of Trustees in 1977. There he heard negative predictions about the future of nonprofit organizations, and he attacked those fears by founding Independent Sector (*Stanford Observer* 1983:3).

The Independent Sector's 1985 Annual Report states its mission: "to create a national forum capable of encouraging the giving, volunteering and not-for-profit initiative that help all of us better serve people, communities and causes." An Evaluation Committee regularly assesses its progress in fulfilling that mission. Its 1985 membership was 650 organizations, a growth of more than 1,000% since its founding, with 53% of the membership comprised of voluntary organizations and 47% of grantmakers. Board members included James A. Joseph, the president of the Council for Foundations, Waldemar A. Nielsen, author of two books about the largest foundations, and J. Richard Wilson, president of the National Society of Fund Raising Executives, Inc.

Independent Sector voting members' dues are one-fourth of 1% of an organization's salaries and benefits on a two-year average for national voluntary organizations. Dues are one-eighth of 1% of the annual grants on a two-year average for foundations and corporations. The maximum dues are $7,000 and the minimum $100. An Associates program is available for $50 to those who do not qualify for voting membership. In addition to membership dues, there is also a Fund for the Future, which had over $2 million in pledges in 1985. The fund includes a program contingency fund and a reserve fund to meet unexpected program costs and to provide for sufficient funding should Independent Sector activities alienate members so that they end their memberships.

Six areas of Independent Sector activity are (1) public information and education, 2) government relations, (3) research, (4) effective sector leadership/management, (5) measurable growth in giving and volunteering, and (6) communications. Independent Sector fosters certain values:

—Commitment beyond self
—Worth and dignity of the individual
—Individual responsibility
—Tolerance
—Freedom
—Justice
—Responsibilities of citizenship

The organization addresses eight problems:

1. Relative decline in giving
2. Encroachments on the freedom of citizens to organize
3. Negative impact of changes in tax policy
4. Greater dependence on government funding by independent institutions
5. Governmental influence on the agenda of the independent sector
6. The limitations of some of the organizations in the sector
7. Limited public understanding of the sector
8. Inadequate recognition of the importance of having alternatives and multiple sources of giving (Payton 1984:6)

In 1986 the National Center for Charitable Statistics, Inc., merged with the Independent Sector, and it acts as a separate program, providing annual financial information from New York, California, New Jersey, and Minnesota, and partial information from Illinois, Indiana, Maryland, Nevada, New Hampshire, Pennsylvania, Virginia, Massachusetts, and Connecticut. Independent Sector has been a leader in activism about issues that affect nonprofit organizations, although its efforts have not always been successful. For instance, it fought to retain the charitable deduction for nonitemizers, but the 1986 tax bill eliminated that deduction. It is sponsoring the "Give 5" or "Daring Goals for a Caring Society" campaign to double charitable giving by 1991.

Independent Sector is also working to counter a 1983 report by the Small Business Administration, "Unfair Competition by Non-profit Organizations with Small Business: An Issue for the 1980s." The report alleges that nonprofits get an unfair competitive advantage by their tax exemptions and that fees for service and other commercial-type activities should disqualify nonprofits from preferential tax treatment. An example of the effect of the report was the loss of the property tax-exempt status of the Portland YMCA because its athletic facilities were alleged to compete unfairly with profit-making health clubs. Independent Sector helped to provide facts about the extent to which unfair competition exists. A 1985 study for Family Service America and the National Assembly of National Voluntary Health and Social Welfare Organizations called the allegation of unfair competition a myth.

Independent Sector, through its predecessor organization Coalition of National Voluntary Organizations, filed an *amicus curiae* brief in February 1980 Supreme Court 8-1 decision of *Village of Schaumburg v. Citizens for a Better Environment et al.* 444 U.S. 620 (1980). The case arose in a Chicago suburb, and the decision recognizes that charitable solicitation is protected as free speech. The Supreme Court ruled that a nonprofit organization may not be denied a solicitation permit simply because its fund raising and administrative costs exceed an arbitrarily established ceiling. The case helped to demonstrate the diversity of funding needs for nonprofits, such as the difference between the needs of a new organization and one that is already established. The decision represents a philosophy of discouraging any arbitrary governmental standards that could be used to stifle the activity of unpopular nonprofit initiatives.

Independent Sector has also encouraged academic programs about philanthropy. One of its early research reports was an overview of the Yale Program on Nonprofit Organizations by the program's director, Professor John Simon. Independent Sector commissioned Robert Payton, president of Exxon Education Foundation, to write a keynote paper for its 1984 annual meeting that included an exhortation to include philanthropy as part of undergraduate education. Independent Sector was also involved in the initial suggestion for Duke University's Center for the Study of Philanthropy.

Regular Independent Sector periodicals are *Memo to Members*, *Government Relations Info and Action*, *Corporate Philanthropy*, *Update* (a summary of materials in *Memo to Members* and *Corporate Philanthropy*), and *Effective Sector Leadership/Management Quarterly*. There are many Independent Sector publications and papers as well as a film, *To Care: America's Voluntary Spirit*. Since 1985, the Independent Sector has published an annual *Resource Directory of Education and Training Opportunities and Other Services*, for nonprofit organizations. The *Directory* includes course descriptions, fees, and scholarship information.

NATIONAL COMMITTEE FOR RESPONSIVE PHILANTHROPY

In 1976 the National Committee for Responsive Philanthropy, having evolved from the Donee Group, began an effort to include smaller, less-established charities in a major $3 million study of philanthropy. The National Committee for Responsive Philanthropy is located at 2001 S Street, N.W., #620, Washington, D.C. 20009, 202-387-9177. Its purpose is to increase philanthropy's accountability to the public and its responsiveness to changing public needs by increasing philanthropy's accessibility to all charities and by increasing the amount of philanthropic dollars going to nontraditional organizations that work "to achieve social justice, equal opportunity and fair representation for disenfranchised people in our economic and governmental systems." The committee's funding comes from membership dues and from private funding sources. The membership dues are available to individuals ($20) and organizations ($20–$200). Dues for organizations are based on the annual income of the organizations, $20 for an income of up to $100,000, $50 for up to $300,000, $100 for up to $500,000, and $200 for greater than $500,000.

The committee monitors several aspects of philanthropy including where philanthropic monies are spent. It reported, for example, that programs for females received less than 4% of the $4.36 billion contributed by foundations in 1984, though that percentage was an improvement from the 1.7% received five years earlier. The committee monitored the percentage of foundation and United Way funding in specific geographic areas going to minority, non-traditional, and new charities, and has found that corporate money often goes to established groups such as the Boy Scouts, local hospitals, and local symphony orchestras.

The committee also monitors the processes that lead to philanthropic decisions as well as those who make the decisions. It encourages philanthropies to provide better reporting to the public by annual reports and public meetings. The committee has criticized the lack of professional staff members in philanthropy, which makes "who you know" more important than what organizations do. It advocates increasing the diversity of philanthropic boards of directors and trustees to include more women and minorities. It has criticized United Way's apparent monopoly of workplace fund raising drives, and it has worked to help several alternative funding organizations compete for payroll deduction contributions. It was an active advocate for more charities to compete in the federal government's annual charity campaign, instead of only the United Way, National Health Agencies, International Service Agencies, and the Red Cross, and it has helped to encourage the creation of alternative new federated campaigns for public employees in several states.

The committee often works through the courts. It filed an *amicus curiae* brief in the Supreme Court decision of *Schaumburg v. Citizens for a Better Environment et al.* which found that laws that restrict an organization's fund raising costs can have a chilling effect on free speech. The brief was filed with Public Citizen, NOW Legal Defense and Education Fund, New York Public Interest Research Group, and the National Black United Fund. The committee also works with legislative and regulatory bodies, testifying before Congress and the IRS on issues such as foundation reporting and regulations for community foundations. It has worked with philanthropic associations and the media as well as internal reform groups such as Women and Foundations/Corporate Philanthropy.

Membership of the committee's Board of Directors indicates the type of organizations that are working to get a better share of philanthropic dollars. The committee's Board Chairpersons have included workers from the National Black United Fund, the Gray Panthers, and the National Council of La Raza. Board members have included workers from the Brown Lung Association, National Association of Social Workers, National Women's Health Network, Sierra Club, Native American Rights Fund, and Vietnam Veterans in America.

The committee publishes a quarterly newsletter, *Responsive Philanthropy* and news bulletins. It holds conferences, and it offers a number of publications. There are several bibliographies available through the committee on such topics as the United Way, lobbying by nonprofit groups, and general readings about philanthropy.

WOMEN AND FOUNDATIONS/CORPORATE PHILANTHROPY

In 1977 an association of women and men grantmakers called Women and Foundations/Corporate Philanthropy organized to help increase foundation and corporate foundation giving to women and girls, as well as to increase the number of female policy makers in philanthropy. The organization is located at 141 Fifth Avenue, Suite 7S, New York, NY 10010, 212-460-9253. Its program includes education, research, networking, and membership development.

Publications by Women and Foundations/Corporate Philanthropy have an impact. An example was a 1981 publication, entitled *Welcome to the Club! (No Women Need Apply)*, about exclusionary practices of private clubs that discriminate for business purposes. The Council on Foundations used the publication in their decision not to use Council on Foundation moneys for dues or program expenses at such clubs, and several foundations adopted similar policies. Another 1981 publication was a public policy statement entitled *Preparing Girls and Young Women for Economic Independence*. The organization circulated it to over two thousand grantmakers in the form of a kit that contained a list of suggestions for the types of programs needed and examples of funded programs.

Women and Foundations/Corporate Philanthropy has no local "chapters." However, networking is one of its program activities.

The organization encourages formal and informal networks among grantmakers in various cities. Networking grantmakers are able to share their insights and experiences with others. Research is another Women and Foundations/Corporate Philanthropy program. One year its Research Committee designed a study of career patterns in philanthropy with funding from the Russell Sage Foundation (Odendah, Boris, Daniels 1985).

WOMEN'S FUNDS

Women's funds are a very recent phenomena in philanthropy. They include four federations that challenge other federated funds, such as the United Way, for workplace fund raising. There are over twenty public or community foundations that make grants to women's organizations, and there are also private foundations that fund women's programs exclusively. Most did not begin with large endowments. They raise their money from personal contact with individuals, direct mail, planned gifts (e.g., securities, life insurance, a trust or bequest in a will), special fund raising events, foundations, and corporations. Many are beginning to build endowments through fund raising that generates enough money to yield high interest when it is invested. There is also a national network of women's funds. The network's national conferences have even attracted participants from women's funds in France and in the Netherlands. The National Committee for Responsive Philanthropy has compiled a comprehensive list of the women's funds (see Appendix).

FUND RAISING EXECUTIVES

The National Society of Fund Raising Executives is the professional organization for fund raising executives. The purpose of NSFRE is "the development and growth of professional fund raising management committed to the preservation and enhancement of the philanthropic process in our society." The address is 1101 King Street, Suite 3000, Alexandria, VA 22314, 703-684-0410. The NSFRE has a Code of Ethics and Professional Practices:

NSFRE: CODE OF ETHICS AND PROFESSIONAL PRACTICES

Preamble

Professional fund raising executives are motivated by positive forces, and by an inner drive to improve the society in which they live through the causes they serve.

They seek to inspire others through their own sense of dedication and high purpose.

They are committed to the improvement of their own professional knowledge and skills in order that their performance will better serve others.

They recognize their trusteeship—to assure their employers that needed resources are rigorously sought, and donors that their purposes in giving are honestly fulfilled.

Such professionals write their own code of ethics every day. Professional Fund-Raising Executives accept and abide by the following Code of Ethics and Professional Practices:

Members shall be responsible for conducting activities in accord with accepted professional standards of accuracy, truth, integrity and good faith.

Members shall encourage institutions they serve: to conduct their affairs in accordance with accepted principles of sound business management, fiduciary responsibility, and accounting procedures; to use donations only for the donors' intended purposes; and to comply with all applicable local, state, provincial and federal laws.

Members shall manage all accounts entrusted to them solely for the benefit of the organizations or institutions being served.

Members shall recommend to the institutions they serve only those fund-raising goals which they believe can be achieved based on their professional experience, and an investigation and rational analysis of facts.

Members shall work for a salary, retainer or fee, not a commission. If employed by a fund-raising organization, that organization shall operate in its client/consultant relationship on the basis of a predetermined fee and not a percentage of the funds raised.

Members shall make full disclosure to employers, clients or, if requested, potential donors, all relationships which might pose, or appear to pose, possible conflicts of interest. As fund-raising executives, they will neither seek nor accept "finder's fees."

Members shall hold confidential and leave intact all lists, records and documents acquired in the service of current or former employers and clients.

A member's public demeanor shall be such as to bring credit to the fund-raising profession. (NSFRE membership brochure)

NSFRE has over 6,500 members. There are more than seventy-five chapters across the United States that offer monthly meetings. There is an annual international conference on fund raising, a newsletter published ten times a year, a journal published twice a year, and the *Quarterly Sightlines*, an issue analysis paper.

NSFRE offers a certification program to its members in the form of a credential for "Certified Fund Raising Executives." The certification program is voluntary, but it demonstrates the efforts of NSFRE to achieve professionalism. Nonmembers are also eligible for certification. A group of certified peers of the applicants reviews their applications for certification. The group ranks each applicant's achievements in terms of fund raising experience for 12–20 points. For example, a director of development receives four points for each year as director. Fund raising courses are worth one point per day including the CASE Workshop, NSFRE Survey course, and planned-giving seminars by Conrad Teitell Institute, Robert F. Sharpe & Co., and Kennedy Sinclaire. Courses worth 1.5 points per continuing education unit are offered by the New School for Social Research, Adelphi University, Fund Raising School, and Southwest Institute. The NSFRE national conference is worth .5 point per day. Fund raising accomplishments may total 15–20 points. For example, each $100,000 raised is worth one point. Post–high school education and continuing professional education is 10–15 points, and a Ph.D. is worth seven points. Service to the profession is worth 8–10 points for activities such as board membership in professional or nonprofit organizations, publications, and teaching.

There is also a four-hour written examination with two hundred multiple-choice questions designed to measure the applicant's knowledge of fund raising principles and techniques. The textbook for preparation for the exam is Dr. Thomas E. Broce's *Fund Raising: The Guide to Raising Money From Private Sources*. The areas covered include prospect-identification, public relations, volunteer leaders, annual giving, direct mail, capital campaigns, planned giving, foundations, corporations, case statements, and ethics.

To be considered for certification, an applicant must have had at least the equivalent of five years of full-time experience as a professinal member of a fund raising staff or as a fund raising consultant to nonprofit organizations, but the experience may be at several institutions. He must also pledge to abide by the NSFRE Code of Ethics and Professional Practices. The application fee is $150. There is no grandfather clause. Those not certified may appeal to the Certification Board. Certification must be renewed every three years for a fee of $30, and the applicant must demonstrate continuous activity in fund raising employment, successful fund raising performance, and continued education and service in the profession. Through the certification program, NSFRE is attempting to educate the public and trustees and directors of nonprofit organizations that there is a need for special training and experience for the management and operation of fund raising programs, and to enlighten the public about the importance of fund raising professionals to the third sector.

CONSULTANTS

A nonprofit voluntary organization's executive director and its board may raise its funds, or the organization may have development officers on its staff. There are also fund raising consultants available who will assist the organization for a fee. In 1935, nine fund raising consultant firms joined together to form the American Association of Fund-Raising Counsel, Inc. (AAFRC).

The AAFRC publishes an annual review of philanthropy, *Giving USA*, and a newsletter, *Fund Raising Review*. State and federal legislatures as well as nonprofit organizations and the general public use these materials often. The American Association of Fund Raising Counsel encourages professional training in fund raising techniques. It also assists in developing laws related to fund raising to help prevent fraudulent practices.

AAFRC standards include the confidentiality of consultations with nonprofit organizations. Counsel members offer initial consultations that are usually without charge. They often recommend a precampaign study to determine whether the client's fund raising goals are feasible and to prepare a fund raising plan. Counsel members provide a detailed budget of the cost of the fund raising program, including fees rather than a percentage or commission.

The 1986 AAFRC Directory lists thirty-two member firms. Most of the firms have several offices across the United States and in Canada. The list includes eleven offices in New York, eight in California, six each in Texas and Illinois, five in New Jersey, four each in Ohio and Massachusetts, three each in Georgia, Pennsylvania, and Missouri, and others in Nebraska, Rhode Island, Connecticut, Washington, D.C., Virginia, Florida, North Carolina, Vermont, Colorado, Oklahoma, and Canada. The AAFRC address is 25 W. Forty-Third Street, New York, NY 10036, 212-354-5799.

There are also nonprofit management consulting organizations that include fund raising ideas in their services. The Support Center is one such organization. It was founded in 1971, and it has a network of twelve offices nationwide. Its headquarters is at 1410 Q Street, N.W., Washington, DC 20009, 202-462-2000. Its resource library contains an affiliate collection of the Foundation Center (a resource center for foundation information) and other fund raising publications. It has its own newsletter, *The Support Center News*. The Support Center offers workshops on topics such as "Fund Raising is More than Passing the Tin Cup," "Board Members as Fund Raisers," "Finding Funding Sources," "Private Foundation Research and Grantwriting," and "How to Ask for Donations in Person with Confidence." Speakers for the workshops include local fund raising experts as well as consultants employed by the Support Center. The Support Center also has an accounting aid program to provide free accounting and financial management assistance to nonprofit organizations.

PERSONAL EXPERIENCES

Certainly philanthropy is essential to the pluralism we enjoy in the United States. We pride ourselves on our diversity, and some claim we are improving our tolerance of the differences between us. Nonprofit organizations are representative of this "melting pot" or "salad bowl" or whatever we call this great blend of citizenry. Nonprofit organizations probably represent every kind of interest group in our society. Their survival depends on continued contributions from individuals, foundations, corporations, and other sources of philanthropy.

One way to encourage U.S. philanthropy is by education. Today there are only a few college courses on fund raising and philanthropy, mostly at the graduate level. Social work schools and business schools both seem obvious settings for curricula in fund raising and philanthropy. I teach an undergraduate course at Oral Roberts University, offered for credit in either social work or business management, though we also have students from other disciplines, such as theology and telecommunication. The course title is "Successful Fund Raising."

I am teaching undergraduates about fund raising because I believe the subject fits what I consider to be the purpose of college education. I was a college student at Stanford during the tumultuous late sixties and early seventies when some of us challenged not only our academic institutions but also the society that supported those institutions. There was regular reference to the concept of "relevance" in college education. When we became adults the colleges and universities we had criticized added us to their alumni lists and wooed us to make contributions. Alumni who are educated about fund raising are potentially not only better contributors to their alma maters but also better contributors to the overall health of society.

The American Association of Colleges selects institutions to receive grants in support of courses about philanthropy. They seek to increase faculty and student awareness of and attention to the significant role philanthropy has played in the social, economic, cultural, and political life of the United States. Initial funding for their grants came from the American Association of Fund-Raising Counsel Trust for Philanthropy, with additional support from Exxon Education Foundation, the J.D.R. 3rd Fund, the National Society of Fund Raising Executives, the Westinghouse Electric Corporation, and Lilly Endowment, Inc. This encouragement is reflective of a growing awareness of the vital importance of fund raising and philanthropy to educational institutions and to our society.

I worked as a contributions analyst at Pennzoil, often dealing with nonprofit organizations whose fund raisers seemed ill-prepared for their jobs. They should have had a college course on the subject. Instead, fund raisers have on-the-job training that consists of "how to" seminars and "how to" books. There is little opportunity for philosophical discussion or debate.

Similarly, those professionals who "give away" money are not academically prepared for their jobs either. They may have on-the-job training, where they learn from their predecessors, or they may rely on self-education. Their opportunities for philosophical discussion and debate are too often limited to talks with their peers among other "donors."

The Independent Sector in Washington, D.C., is one of the leaders in trying to bridge the gaps that exist in the education of "fund raisers" and "fund givers." Robert L. Payton, who wrote the keynote paper for the Independent Sector's 1984 annual meeting, has corresponded with me and encouraged me very much in my teaching of this topic to undergraduates, and I have used his papers in my course. He has also encouraged me in writing this book.

I chose the title "Successful Fund Raising" for my course because I felt it would have more appeal to students shopping for an elective. The course is offered for credit in either social work or business management, but it also includes material about philanthropy from the disciplines of political science, history, theology, and communication. It is indeed interdisciplinary, and one of the assets of the course is the opportunity for interaction between students from majors as varied as social work and business.

In addition to my "Successful Fund Raising" course at ORU, I have had many informal consulting sessions with students, faculty, and staff to discuss various funding projects for nonprofit organizations in which they are involved. Several of these people are the founders of their own agencies or are planning their own agencies. Some are involved in ORU's many missions projects, especially during the summers.

An assignment for the students in my course is to prepare a case statement and an outline of a proposal for funding an already existing agency of their choice. The students choose social welfare agencies, cultural organizations, or church projects. They anonymously critique one another's proposals, and I critique all of the proposals, thus acting somewhat in a consulting role. I have also offered fund raising seminars to the public. These have been small, and they have sometimes resulted in informal consultations.

One summer I worked in Washington, D.C., for two controversial organizations, Dr. Ernest Lefever's Ethics and Public Policy Center and Reverand Jerry Falwell's Moral Majority. I was hired by fund raisers at each organization, although my duties were more specifically in fund raising at the Ethics and Pubic Policy Center. I worked there with Dan Bonner, who was formerly with Chase

Manhattan Bank's contribution program. That summer Dr. Lefever was embroiled in the controversy surrounding his nomination by President Reagan to be Assistant Secretary for Human Rights and Humanitarian Affairs. I was paid an honorarium by the Ethics and Public Policy Center. My consulting consisted of reviewing its lists of donors, researching the *Foundation Directory* regarding potential donors, and making recommendatinos concerning corporate donors, particularly in Texas and Oklahoma. As with all my informal consulting recommendations, though, I emphasized the importance of individual donors, beginning with the members of the Board of Directors and their acquaintances.

2

Individuals

INTRODUCTION

In the first session of my "Successful Fund Raising" class I instruct the students to draw a circle on a piece of paper and to divide the circle into three sections, labeling each section as it represents their guess as to the percentages of all U.S. philanthropy that come from (1) individuals, (2) foundations, and (3) corporations. Individuals are single people and families who contribute to nonprofit organizations. Foundations are legally created entities required to donate a certain percentage of their assets to nonprofit organizations. Corporations are profit-making entities allowed to give contributions to nonprofit organizations.

No student has ever guessed correctly. In fact, the students' guesses are usually just the opposite of the correct percentages. For 1985 the American Association of Fund-Raising Counsel reported in *Giving USA* that the percentages were 89.2% individuals and bequests, 5.4% foundations, and 5.4% corporations (The Support Center 1986:2). The students usually guess that foundations and corporations give the greatest percentages and that individuals give the least. They are wrong. Individuals give the greatest amount of money to nonprofit organizations. That principle is fundamental to successful fund raising. *People give to people.*

Whether gifts are solicited by the organization's executive director, volunteers on its Board of Directors, or hired fund raisers, the concept of "people give to people" is involved. Do those people soliciting funds have the interpersonal communication skills that make them effective in raising money? Do their personalities click with their prospective donors?

Some organizations hold campaigns where they try to match donors and solicitors. The board members brainstorm about their acquaintances who are prospects for gifts. Some of these prospects, once they have given, are asked to help with further prospecting. Each individual solicits four or five others who, in turn, solicit four or five others. The ethical issues in such campaigns include confidentiality. Should a board member who is a bank president publicize his big accounts as prospects to board members?

The social implications of this process are obvious: "I'll give to your fund drive for Charity X if you'll give to my fund drive for Charity Y." Does that mean that all fund raising begins on the golf course or at a social function or funding event? What about fund raisers who don't belong to that social class? If there is no milieu where both the fund raiser and the prospective donor are comfortable, perhaps that fund raiser is not the one to solicit that gift. If the fund raiser is simply pursuing the satisfaction of "rubbing shoulders with the rich and famous," then he will be doing the organization a disservice, because his own goals will have priority over the organization's. If he is merely trying to increase his personal power or popularity in the organization by bringing in money, the prospective donors he solicits may discern his motives and choose not to be a means to the ends he seeks.

The political ramifications of the concept of "people give to people" are also noteworthy. It is possible for the gifts of individuals in a community to be given to only a few select organizations. For example, some people may give to cultural organizations merely because they like to publicize their names in the program given to the audience at cultural events. Other givers may be wary of new or controversial organizations.

It is important to recognize that it usually takes years to build a strong base of support among individuals. The time used in such cultivation will bear fruit of great rewards in the future of the organization. A final question is, therefore, how long does the organization plan to exist?

MOTIVATIONS FOR CONTRIBUTIONS

In 1985 the Rockefeller Brothers Fund commissioned a nationwide study by Yankelovich, Skelly and White, Inc., entitled *The Charitable Behavior of Americans*. Over 1,100 adults participated in the research. The study confirmed that the most effective fund raising technique is one person asking another for a contribution. This approach works best among larger donors if the person requesting the donation and the donor are already well acquainted (White 1986:3). People do indeed give to people.

These research findings also begin to provide a key to understanding what motivates people to make contributions. Factors that influenced their charitable giving include income level, life experience, age, religious involvement, and marital status. The person most likely to give a higher percentage of his income as contributions is thirty-five to sixty-four years old, married, and earns more than $50,000. The person least likely to contribute is over sixty-five years old, separated or divorced, and earning $10,000 or less. Thirty-eight percent of the individuals in the study felt they should give more contributions, but some either did not get around to it (23%) or were not asked to make a contribution (14%). Giving is also affected by how much money individuals feel they have to spend. More people with incomes higher than $50,000 believe they have discretionary income than do those with incomes less than $10,000. However, only 25% of those under thirty-five years old who have moderate discretionary income donate 3% or more of their income, compared to forty% of those individuals with moderate discretionary income over thirty-five years old (White 1986:2).

The study found a positive correlation between volunteerism and giving donations. Twenty-six percent of all those surveyed gave 3% or more of their incomes as contributions. Nearly 60% of those were active as volunteers, compared to 47% of all the respondents. A related finding was that 62% of those in the survey preferred giving in their own communities (White 1986:2–3). Both the research finding about the relation of volunteerism to giving and the finding about the preference for community giving also support the idea that people give to people because the donors are more likely to know the people who benefit from their contributions.

The study also ranked the appeal that nonreligious organizations have to individual donors. Individuals respond in the following order: United Way (federated campaigns), medical, social welfare, international, colleges and universities, public radio/television, hospitals, environmental charities, etc. However, the mean contributions to these recipient groups are in a different rank order: colleges and universities ($270); educational charities ($250); United Way ($210); hospitals ($170); social welfare ($150), and medical ($90). The impetus for gifts to nonreligious organizations is varied. 40% of those individuals who make total annual contributions of $500 or more either do so without being asked or they are solicited by their acquaintances. Forty percent respond to an advertisement. Thirty percent respond to direct mail from colleges or universities. Twenty-one percent give to the United Way through their employer's campaign. The gifts are also sporadic. Only 11% of those who give to nonreligious organizations attempt to give a fixed percentage of their annual incomes, and only 5% have decided a total amount to give annually (White 1986:7).

Individual giving in this country can be increased, and education about philanthropy is necessary to help bring about that increase. U.S. citizens give an average of 2.4% of their income to charities. Those individuals under thirty-five years old, who give the least, need education about philanthropy to help them give a greater percentage of their incomes to charity. Overall, there needs to be an educational campaign to encourage those individuals already making contributions and those individuals who would like to give more.

What motivates an individual to contribute? The psychology of giving is a relatively new field of study. The concept behind "people give to people" is that individual donors are motivated to make a contribution because of their relationship to the individual who solicits their gift. They must trust and respect that individual. Perhaps the solicitor personifies the organization to the potential donor. Perhaps the donor gives because he respects the solicitor or owes him a favor. If so, the best solicitors would be those capable of a quid pro quo relationship with the donor, those who could say, "I'll give to your nonprofit project if you'll give to mine." Sometimes it is difficult for acquaintances to be explicit about fund raising, though, and donations are lost if there is an awkwardness between solicitor and donor when they discuss money. Nonetheless, some fund raisers suggest that the solicitor and donor should at least be of comparable wealth.

There is no guarantee that wealthy individuals will be generous philanthropists. One study by a college development officer found that of 184 publicly reported gifts made in 1985 valued at a million dollars or more, only twenty-two were made by individuals whom *Forbes* magazine listed among the four hundred wealthiest people in the United States, or approximately 12%. The study further delineated the areas of these gifts. Less than 10% of the six-figure gifts to education came from donors on the *Forbes* list, two out of twelve such gifts to hospitals and health care, one of the six large gifts to the arts and humanities, and three of the eight such gifts to civic and public causes. The study does not, however, account for gifts of less than $1 million by the wealthy, and it acknowledges that its source, *Giving USA*, published by the American Association of Fund-Raising Counsel, may have missed some large gifts (*Fund Raising Management* 1987d:6).

BOARDS OF DIRECTORS

Although the nation's wealthiest individuals may not make all of the gifts of over $1 million to nonprofit organizations, wealthy individuals are necessary as members of nonprofit boards. Must every board member make a monetary contribution? A standard response is that every board member must "give, get, or get off." In other words, each board member must either give money or successfully solicit money. Many contributors will give money only when the board members have all given. Yet some nonprofit administrators dislike the "give, get, or get off" idea. Social service administrators particularly would rather have participative management in which the board members include people who received social service from the agency, and often these recipients do not have money to give nor do they know anyone they could solicit for funds. Generally, however, the economic reality is that most social service agencies must have board members who will "give, get, or get off." Dr. Tom Broce, author of the text used by the National Society of Fund Raising Executives, suggests that the board give 20% and that the next 20% come from those next closest to the organization (Broce 1986:46).

Board members are volunteers. As board members they are also legally responsible for the actions of the organization. It is wise to provide insurance for board members. They must disclose all possible conflicts of interest. There should be an attorney on the board and one retained separately to handle legal issues. The treasurer of the board should be bonded as should any other members handling money.

In most nonprofit voluntary organizations, board members hire and fire the executive director. The potential for power struggles is obvious. If a board member is the largest individual donor to the organization, do her opinions automatically have the greatest influence and sway the other board members? Could powerful board members lead an organization into activities that are outside of its founding purpose? Could the board even fire the founder of the organization? To try to avoid these conflicts, it is crucial that each board member understand the *raison d'être*, the reason for being, of the organization. What is its purpose? Why does it exist? Once board members understand the mission, or reason for being, of the organization, they will be better able to decide the extent of their contributions of money, time, and expertise.

The proper care and utilization of board members is vital to the success of any nonprofit organization. Jerry A. Linzy, a past chairman of the National Association for Hospital Development with nearly twenty years experience as a development officer, met with thirty leaders in his community and discussed what they looked for in nonprofit organizations that sought their time, expertise, and money. The leaders represented businesses with from 20 to 1,000 employees, with annual revenues ranging from $5 million to $25 million. All of the leaders acknowledged the need for fund raising in nonprofit organizations, and though most of them did not want to be fund raisers, the fund raising dimension was not a deterrent to their participation. The group recommended that those seeking volunteer leaders should begin with the leaders they have, asking them to identify other leaders. The group encouraged nonprofits to realize that it is important to a volunteer to have friends already involved in the program. Linzy suggests there be a complete discussion of fund raising responsibilities, before an individual volunteers for the board, as part of any recruitment effort. Linzy likens recruiting board members to obtaining a major funding gift—proper "cultivation" of the prospective board members is necessary. Even if an individual declines joining the board, that person will have at least been made aware of the program.

Once a person agrees to join the board it is important to provide useful orientation. Linzy suggests that the person should certainly be included on the mailing list for important mailings. He also suggests that another board member be assigned to welcome the new member and answer questions. There should also be a formal orientation to introduce the new member to the staff and to the workings of the organization.

Linzy's mini-survey found several reasons why individuals drop out of board memberships. One reason was boredom. They did not enjoy being underutilized. It was also important for them to have a specific task. On the other hand, some dropped out because they felt there had been a misrepresentation to them of what was expected in terms of time and/or fund raising. Some left simply because they were not having fun (*Fund Raising Management* 1987c:60).

The precious commodity the volunteer offers is time. All volunteers in this country volunteered $70 billion worth of time in 1984 (Bonjean 1986:3). Each board member's time should be valued and respected. For example, sometimes a conference call will accomplish as much as a formal committee meeting, eliminating the time spent traveling to meeting sites. If a board has always met according to a certain schedule, that schedule could be re-evaluated. Is each meeting truly necessary? Could several meetings be combined into a board retreat? Also, is every committee really necessary? Does each committee fit the broader mission of the organization?

Every board member should be involved in fund raising. As with all board activities, each fund raising activity should be essential or it should be eliminated. For example, many organizations conduct role-playing sessions to help train board members and other volunteers to ask for contributions. Perhaps the same training could be available in the form of a training manual. The board members could be queried about their fund raising experience, and the training could be provided according to their unique needs.

There should be recognition and awards for the board members' accomplishments in behalf of the nonprofit organization. If the board is willing, fund raising activities can encourage competition between various committees. Social events too should increase the board's enthusiasm.

"CAMPAIGNS" AND "EVENTS" FOR BOARD MEMBERS AND VOLUNTEERS

The cover story of the January 1987 *Fund Raising Management* magazine describes a fund raising campaign to raise over $143 million for a performing arts center in Orange County, California. This campaign demonstrates excellent utilization of individual volunteers and contributors. First, there was a lead gift of land valued at $6 million for the site and a $6 million cash contribution from the same family. The consulting company that conducted the fund raising campaign had personal interviews with over one hundred potential major donors, and they learned that those individuals were not confident about the original board of directors' ability to raise the funds. Moreover, there was concern that the original board would not have time for fund raising because of their other responsibilities regarding the new center. Therefore, the bylaws of the organization were amended to allow the creation of a board standing committee solely responsible for raising the money for the new center. Although the standing committee retained the voting rights and privileges of board members, they were not required to attend board meetings.

There was competition between various phases of the fund raising campaign. There was also public recognition and personal acknowledgment of volunteer accomplishments. The campaign lasted six years, and the seven full-time fund raising staff and ten support staff attempted to do 90% of the work, whereas the volunteers did the crucial 10% of the work—the actual solicitation of contributions. There were many social events and public ceremonies throughout to maintain the enthusiasm of the volunteers (*Fund Raising Management* 1987b:28).

Many nonprofit organizations use similar strategies for fund raising for buildings, or for capital campaigns. The volunteer solicitors are divided into groups to solicit distinct sets of donors, such as major donors, in phases throughout the campaign. There is a targeted amount of money to be raised from each set of donors. In the Orange County Arts Center campaign, each phase of the campaign began once there was assurance that the preceding phase was successful, thus helping to maintain an optimistic enthusiasm throughout (*Fund Raising Management* 1987b:28).

On a smaller level a "picnic" funding event raised $10,000 for Domestic Violence Intervention Services in Tulsa, Oklahoma. The chairperson, Mrs. Ann Fields, had lived in Tulsa nine years. She served five years, or more than one term, on the Board of Directors for Domestic Violence Intervention Services. She was first recruited for the board by a colleague at Arthur Andersen where she was an audit manager responsible for the supervision of thirty-five employees. She is a certified public accountant with a bachelor's degree in accounting from Oklahoma State University.

Mrs. Fields became chairperson of the picnic just six weeks before the event was held, replacing the former chairperson. Her predecessor had selected the volunteers on her committee. Mrs. Fields did not know two-thirds of the volunteers when she became chairperson.

At her first meeting with the committee the members brainstormed to determine the priority of activities. Preparation of five thousand invitations was the most pressing need. Her committee consisted of subcommittees, such as Decorations, Silent Auction, Arrangements (for a "liquor license" and insurance, etc.). Each subcommittee was composed of volunteers. Mrs. Fields had prior experience on church committees, but this was her first volunteer leadership position. She found it quite different from working with those she had supervised at Arthur Andersen, who were used to being assigned tasks and to having regular performance appraisals. If a volunteer did not perform a task, Mrs. Fields learned she would have to do it herself or recruit someone else. When she became chairperson of the funding event she was a new mother and no longer employed at Arthur Andersen, where she had had easy access to secretarial assistance and to the corporate word processing center. Arthur Andersen strongly encourages its employees to participate in volunteer civic activities, and the corporation is flexible in allowing work time to be used for those activities.

It was helpful to Mrs. Fields that her committee included the chairperson of the picnic event from the previous year and a few volunteers who had served on the committee the last year. She was able to learn from them. However, she also decided to keep a written notebook for her own successor to use the next year. The notebook includes an outline of each step of the event, such as information about solicitations for money and for in-kind donations for the Silent Auction. She also provided suggestions for the event, such as the need to review the criteria for issuing complimentary tickets.

More people had attended the preceding year, the first year of the event, but the net amount of money raised was about the same because more complimentary tickets had been given the first year. There was no budget for the event per se, but about $3,000 in corporate donations was raised by another committee before the event. The corporate donors were given blocks of complimentary tickets for their employees. Mrs. Fields felt there was a need to improve fiscal control. Tickets to the event were sold for $25. There was a computerized list of those who purchased advance tickets. No record was kept of those who purchased tickets at the door for cash. Otherwise, a record could have been made from the checks. The tax deduction for the tickets came through using the canceled check as a receipt. Ten percent of the money raised was used to reimburse out-of-pocket expenses. Ninety percent of the cost, however, was donated, such as the room for the event and the food.

Mrs. Fields felt that the low ebb in the Tulsa economy may have affected the event. More specifically, though, she did not learn until one week before the event that another major funding event was scheduled for the very same night by the American Diabetes Association. It was a $200-a-plate black-tie dinner that included a roast of one of the state's senators, and it was held directly across the street from her picnic. This scheduling conflict could have been avoided by checking the calendar of the Tulsa Arts and Humanities Council earlier.

Mrs. Fields has other suggestions. She suggests an early start for preparation for the event. She also recommends better publicity.

Finally, she suggests recruiting a name entertainer to help draw a bigger crowd. In the meantime, Mrs. Fields will continue to serve on the board and will be available to offer advice to the next chairperson of the picnic funding event.

THE JUNIOR LEAGUE

In 1901 Mary Harriman founded the nation's first Junior League in New York to help the poor and to assist "young women of means in search of moral purpose." She and a group of her friends volunteered at the New York College Settlement with the goal "to unite for a definite purpose the debutantes of each season and to interest the young women of New York in the work of the Settlement Movement." They raised $1,500 the first year for a gymnasium and an art school at the Settlement House. There were also committees to work in the Settlement House library, to redecorate one of the rooms, to teach art and modeling, to send flowers to the poor and sick, and to provide music for the kindergarten children and young married women. In 1907 the group changed its name to The Junior League for the Promotion of Neighborhood Work. By 1912 there were Junior League chapters in several cities. The League provided Red Cross volunteers during both world wars.

Today the League is active in current issues, and even government officials seek to know the League's viewpoint. There are 160,000 women in 266 locations across the country. The New York League has projects to provide transitional housing for homeless families, to train women to set up child care facilities in their own homes, to teach English to immigrants, to monitor legislation about domestic violence and child abuse, to offer skills workshops to women in prison, to promote community awareness of rape, to promote reproductive choice and women's rights, to visit children facing long-term hospitalization, to provide education about alcoholism and about Alzheimer's Disease, and to help prevent teen pregnancies. One year of the New York Junior League's fund raising calendar included a holiday boutique in October, a Thanksgiving Eve Ball in November where they introduced college-age provisional members, a Winter Ball, and two mini–fund raisers: a reception to benefit their Alzheimer's Disease brochure and a spring boutique to benefit their Shelter Task Force. The New

York Junior League has given development training to all of its committee chairpersons. It is attempting to enlighten all of its members about the potential for corporate and foundation funding and is encouraging greater member involvement in development to increase the number of contacts in the community. There is a Fund Raising Vice President and a Fund Raising Manager on the Board of Managers.

The Junior League is a charitable nonprofit volunteer organization. It offers volunteers who work in cooperation with public and private agencies to provide ongoing services and to develop demonstration projects to meet community needs. It also seeks training from experts in the community. For example, the New York Junior League invited a social work professor from Columbia University to conduct role-playing discussions with the League's Shelter Task Force to help the Task Force members in their work with homeless families. Other social work faculty have led discussions about political advocacy for the homeless, demographics, child abuse, mental illness, addiction, and teen pregnancy.

In the New York Junior League there are over 2,600 trained women volunteers. Eighty-five percent are employed full-time or part-time. One-third have children. It would be interesting to query whether Junior League members motivate donors to contribute simply by their own elite social status and personalities or by their relating to the plights of the people they help. The "Lady Bountiful" image can mean direct volunteer service as well as money contributions through their fund raising balls and boutiques.

Across the country Junior Leagues have different attitudes toward the Lady Bountiful image. The New York Junior League deliberately avoids it. Membership is open to any woman between eighteen and thirty-nine years old who is able to fulfill a required time commitment of at least two and a half hours per week. The New York Junior League includes members who are bankers, attorneys, and officers of corporations, but none in the more traditional professions such as nursing and teaching. Unlike Leagues in other parts of the country, it has no thrift shops or tearooms. The New York League does not raise funds for other nonprofits, preferring hands-on involvement.

Because of the professional composition of the New York Junior League, however, it has had to develop policies about the use of the League for professional networking by members. There is no formal mechanism for networking, such as a directory categorizing members according to their professions. In fact, the League will not provide information about other members' professions to members who are merely seeking employment opportunities (Swan 1987).

DIRECT MAIL

Mail solicitations are second only to personal contact by acquaintances as the most effective fund raising techniques (White 1986:4). Telethons, radiothons, telephone appeals, and media advertising are all less effective than direct mail. The success of the Live Aid concert/telethon in raising $35 to $70 million in gifts and pledges for international famine relief was merely the result of the responsiveness of individuals under thirty years old and of individuals with incomes over $50,000 in international philanthropy (White 1986:4).

Many organizations use fund raising letters to build their constituency of individual donors. The standard response to direct mail is only about 2% of those who receive the letters. Is this method illustrative of the concept that "people give to people"? Don't most people throw away their "junk mail"?

The direct mail method of solicitation does arise from the concept of "people give to people." Fund raising letters try to communicate individual personalities. Such letters may carry personal signatures. The latest laser technology is capable of reproducing "personalized" letters complete with digitized signatures. Of course, there are ethical issues involved in the use of direct mail. For example, is the "personalization" of the letters deceptive? Do the letters falsely claim that there is a funding emergency? Do the letters manipulate vulnerable recipients, such as lonely people who don't receive much mail, particularly elderly widows and widowers?

The resolution of each of these ethical issues is simply to tell the truth. The first issue—of whether the "personalization" of such letters is deceptive—has been resolved by organizations that, for example, routinely carry an article in their magazine or newsletter about their computer mail departments, including pictures of the

people who work there. They may list the steps in the direct mail
process: what happens when the reply letters are opened, who ca-
tegorizes the responses, who helps in the printing of the fund raising letters.

The issue of false emergency funding letters is similarly resolved
by truthfulness. An emergency must be proven by additional information. What is the budget of the organization? How much
money is in reserve or endowments? How far short of the budget
is the income, and is the shortfall a seasonal one that will probably be resolved before the year ends?

The issue of manipulation of vulnerable recipients of the letters
again enters the pioneer territory of the psychology of giving. Is
everyone manipulated by what they read? Is the letter's success
based on whether the letter arrived in the mailbox on a busy mail
day, such as a birthday, or on a slow mail day, or on payday?
There are fund raising consultants who study the most successful
funding letters: what color paper has the best appeal, what size
type works best, what length of letter is most effective, should
there be a stamped return envelope, etc. Are these physical characteristics of the letter determinative?

Fund raisers may purchase names on mailing lists from profit-
making direct mail companies who sell such lists. Some provide
demographic data with the names. Some provide information about
pledges, gifts, and other donor histories. Fund raising magazines
carry direct mail company advertisements. They also provide names
of list compilers and owners, mailing list brokers, mailing list
managers, and computerized donor file services. It is unethical for
a nonprofit organization to sell or provide names and addresses of
its own donors to another nonprofit organization. On the other
hand, a nonprofit organization should be diligent in recording the
names and addresses of all those individuals who have expressed
an interest in the organization in any way. Each individual's history of giving to the organization should be recorded. The most
obvious method of centralized record keeping is computers. This
raises the additional ethical issue of the confidentiality of information.

Postal rates are another important issue affecting direct mail.
From 1980 to 1986, basic nonprofit third-class rates rose 174%.
In October 1986 Congress passed legislation to freeze the rate for

one year. The same bill also required a recalculation of "revenue foregone" appropriations to reimburse the postal service for its overhead while nonprofits pay only the direct cost of mail. The provision assures stable or even declining rates after January 1989. The arguments for cheaper nonprofit rates and for lowering the revenue foregone appropriation to the postal service are that nonprofit mail is presorted, it is generally of uniform size, it is processed at nonpeak times, and the postal service may send it more slowly through the mail system.

DEFERRED/PLANNED GIVING

Most nonprofit organizations eventually begin planned giving programs, in which the donor receives some life income and/or designates that a contribution occur after his death. It is essential that the organization be aware of the most recent tax law changes affecting these programs. If the organization does not have an attorney on its development staff, it should be prepared to retain a tax attorney for guidance. In addition, the organization should insist that all donors to the program retain their own attorneys. If a donor does not have an attorney, the organization should recommend an experienced estate planning attorney and also recommend that the donor deduct the attorney's fee from his contribution.

A donor may make a contribution that pays him an income for life. The various life income plans are charitable remainder annuity trusts, charitable remainder unitrusts, pooled income funds, charitable gift annuities, deferred payment gift annuities, and donation of real estate while retaining life ownership of it.

The charitable remainder annuity trust is the irrevocable transfer of assets to a trust fund. The trust principal becomes the property of the nonprofit organization. The donor or his designated beneficiary receives a fixed amount of money annually. If the trust's annual income is not sufficient to pay the fixed amount, the trustee for the fund must pay the difference out of trust principal or capital gains. The donor receives an income tax deduction based on his age. U.S. Treasury Department tables specify the amount the donor may deduct.

The charitable remainder unitrust is an irrevocable transfer of assets to a trust fund that pays the donor a fixed percentage of the fair market value of the assets of the trust. The percentage may not be less than 5%, and the value of the trust is redetermined each year. Thus, a $200,000 gift at 5% would result in $10,000 income the first year, and $12,500 the second year if the trust assets have been revalued at $250,000. The donor's tax deduction is based on his age. It is possible to invest the trust assets so that part of each payment can be taxed at a lower capital gains rate.

Pooled income funds are particularly popular planned giving programs among universities. The university or other nonprofit organization invests the donor's irrevocable gift of money or securities in a pool of other similar gifts. The donors annually receive their pro rata share of the income of the pooled trust. The donor's tax deduction is determined by his age and the pool's earning experience. At Stanford University, for example, about half of Stanford's three hundred life income gifts go into two pooled income funds. Its Pooled Income Fund I, with a 16.46% per year return, was in the top 5% nationally compared to pension fund managers of balanced funds. The total 1985 return (yield plus appreciation) was almost 20% (*Stanford Observer* 1986b:17).

The charitable gift annuity is an irrevocable gift of money or securities to the nonprofit organization. The nonprofit organization then pays the donor or a designated beneficiary an annuity of fixed annual payment for life. The annual rates of return are the same for men and women. A portion of the annuity payment is tax-free.

The deferred payment gift annuity payment is designed for the donor who wants to guarantee his income after retirement. He makes the gift before retirement and immediately saves taxes accordingly. However, his annuity payments do not begin until his retirement or a date he specifies.

A donor may also donate real estate to a nonprofit organization but retain use of the property for the rest of his lifetime or the lifetime of his survivor, if desired. There is an immediate charitable tax deduction in the year of the gift. The deduction is based on the donor's age and the value of the real estate. The donor also receives the same estate tax benefits as if he had made a bequest. There will be a savings of probate cost as well.

In addition to such planned gifts that provide income, there are also contributions specified in wills. The federal tax laws and many state tax laws allow an estate tax charitable deduction for such gifts. Estate tax payments are based on the size of the estate after such contributions have been made.

Planned gift programs must meet several legal and ethical requirements. There must be an absence of conflict of interest in the investment decisions for the various funds. Of course, there is a fiduciary responsibility to the donor. There should be regular audits of the funds and reports to donors. There should be prompt payment to all donors. The Board of Directors must be annually apprised of the performance of the funds. Any person who makes an irrevocable gift to a nonprofit organization should also have sufficient assets to provide for himself and his heirs, or his gift should be discouraged. The program should be conducted professionally with dignity and integrity.

Stanford University is first in gift support among private universities in this country. For its 1985–1986 fiscal year, individual donors gave $72.4 million, and bequests totalled $36 million. The University Treasurer's Office manages and invests about $142 million in trust accounts for people who have given life income gifts to Stanford. The university often gets a higher return on investments than the donors were getting when they managed their own assets. One widow, for example, irrevocably donated her shares of IBM stock, which had given her a 4% return. The university sold the stock and reinvested the proceeds in stocks and bonds to pay the widow a 7.5% return. Stanford also strives to maintain a personal relationship with the life income beneficiaries through its employees in the Trust Services Office. They send the beneficiaries a check and personal letter every quarter. In turn, some of the beneficiaries correspond with the Trust Services Office, even sending updates on their grandchildren, etc. (*Stanford Observer* 1986b:17).

Stanford has used professionals to manage its trusts since the 1960s, when the Ford Foundation so recommended for all universities. Stanford was one of the first universities to establish written, explicit investment guidelines. One goal is to maintain the purchasing power of the endowment over time, and the University

Treasurer believes that not much more than 5% of principal should be consumed each year to avoid consuming real principal (*Stanford Observer* 1986a:15).

Stanford invests in nontraditional assets such as venture capital and international securities, believing these to produce higher returns than other stocks. About 8% of the endowment is invested in venture capital, backing individuals who have formed professional venture capital partnerships as well as directly investing. There was a 56% return in 1984, but a minus 13% return in 1985 due to the problems in Silicon Valley. About 10% of the endowment is invested in international securities, particularly in the Pacific Basin because the United States dropped from 70% of the world's GNP in 1970 to 50% in 1980, whereas there was great growth in the Pacific Basin. The university also invested in international bonds just as the value of the U.S. dollar was peaking (*Stanford Observer* 1986a:15).

Stanford investments also include domestic stocks and bonds, real estate and oil, gas, gold, silver, and other minerals. About 40% of the endowment is invested in large capitalization domestic stock, with most of that managed by Capital Guardian Trust Co. Stanford uses such outside portfolio managers to handle most of its endowment. It chose Capital Guardian Trust Co. because Capital is owned by the people who work there and because Capital spends more money on research than do most investment institutions. A licensed real estate broker on the Stanford staff handles transactions involving its 160 gift properties, valued at $25 million. A minerals administrator handles oil, gas, and mineral leases that yield over $2 million a year. A Petroleum Investment Committee, made up of graduates and friends of the School of Earth Science, manages the Petroleum Investment Fund that acquires oil properties (*Stanford Observer* 1986a:15).

EFFECTS OF THE 1986 TAX ACT

The 1986 tax legislation was the first complete overhaul of the tax system since 1954. The new law, effective once President Reagan signed it on Wednesday morning, October 22, 1986, includes several sections that affect charitable giving by individuals. The most publicized is the elimination of the charitable deduction for nonitemizers. The 1981 Tax Act had allowed nonitemizer taxpayers in 1982 and 1983 to deduct a maximum of $25 of their charitable contributions. It allowed nonitemizers in 1984 to deduct a maximum of $75 of their charitable contributions. In 1985 they could deduct half of their contributions, and in 1986 they could deduct all of their contributions. The provision was scheduled to "sunset," or end, in 1986 unless Congress renewed it, but the 1986 Act did not renew it. The deduction for itemizers remains, but it is less valuable due to the slash in tax rates.

Lowered tax rates raise the cost of charitable gifts. Before the 1986 law, individuals in the highest tax bracket of 50% saved 50 cents in taxes for every dollar they gave to nonprofit organizations. Once the 1986 law is fully implemented, their savings will be only 28 cents on the dollar.

Another change for individual contributors is that some gifts of appreciated property may be subject to the alternative minimum tax for the value of the appreciated portion. Otherwise the same rules apply as before: there is no tax on the appreciated portion, and the individual may claim deduction on the fair market value of the property. The change will generally affect only very large gifts of appreciated property by very high-income individuals because the appreciation can be added to their tax preference items subject to the alternative minimum tax. Yet many middle-income individuals can now make gifts of appreciated property that cost less than under the prior law. Also large gifts of appreciated property such as stocks can be spread over several years to avoid the minimum tax.

PERSONAL EXPERIENCES

One of my guest speakers in my "Successful Fund Raising" class at Oral Roberts University told the class that most people begin their fund raising from individuals early in childhood, when they solicit their parents for extra money for themselves. Later, children may join other children to raise money for special projects. They may be recruited by adults to go door-to-door selling something for the contribution: Scout cookies, Camp Fire candy, school band calendars, etc. Each solicitation involves some sort of personal interaction with the donor. I participated in many of these fund raising activities growing up. Later, in graduate school, I was the coordinator for the UNICEF fund drive at the University of Texas, the annual Halloween fund raiser for UNICEF. I wrote articles in the university paper, and I met with representatives from the dorms and the Greeks, like the Inter-Fraternity Council, to encourage individual gifts to UNICEF and to encourage social activity fund raisers to benefit UNICEF. To motivate students to participate I related my personal experiences working with undernourished children when I was a teen volunteer in an innoculation program in villages in Honduras and Guatemala.

I also had experience in individual philanthropy in my work with the A.D. Players, a Christian theatre company in Houston. The Players have a significant number of individual donors. I worked with the direct mail program, sorting letters by zip code, helping make decisions about the use of postage-paid return envelopes, etc. There were also memorial donations. I drafted the various thank-you letters and worked with the company's founder and the Chairman of the Board of Directors regarding the more personal acknowledgments. I was also an actress and singer with the company. We Players were the guests one weekend at a brunch given by Ruth and June Hunt, the widow and daughter of the late H. L. Hunt, at the Hunt home in Dallas that is modeled after Mount Vernon. Despite the famed Hunt wealth, I found it interesting to see the phrase "just plain folks" among their home furnishings.

When I worked as a contributions analyst at Pennzoil, I joined the board of Houston's Camp Fire. I had been a Camp Fire Girl for many years while growing up, but I knew my appointment to the Houston Board was more the result of my job at Pennzoil. At that time, the Camp Fire board was embarking on a $1.5 million capital campaign.

When I discuss the interpersonal aspect of philanthropy with the students in my "Successful Fund Raising" class, I believe the students and I all deal at some level with our own upbringings and our attitudes about personal wealth. These affect our attitudes toward discussing money. Indeed this self-awareness may be embarrassing, and I do not ask the students to make their own revelations public.

I do indulge in a few personal stories that give them hints about my own attitudes toward personal wealth. Certainly these stories

allow me at least to "name drop," but it would be better to use
the stories as a means to delve into the psychological and sociological motivations for "name dropping." These stories could also
cause the students to consider the relationship between wealth,
status, and power in the United States. Do the students desire wealth
for themselves? Do they desire to marry someone who is as wealthy
as they are? Does money matter? Do they feel it is "filthy lucre,"
and do they, therefore, feel self-righteous toward those who are
wealthy? On the other hand, if they consider themselves wealthy,
how comfortable are they with their wealth? Do they act competitive about their wealth compared to others? Are they suspicious
of people who want to be their friends? How does a person publicize that he is wealthy: by his family, by his possessions, by the
schools he attends? What about eccentrics? If the students have
wealthy friends, are they able to talk about money with these
friends? Would they be able to ask their acquaintances to give
money to a project? Do they seek friends among the nonwealthy?
For many people there is an awkward ambivalence toward interpersonal interactions in which they may eventually request a donation from the other person for some pet project. Does the other
person become a "means to an end" for them rather than an end
in themselves?

Most people are aware of the many ethical issues involving the
use of direct mail. As a faculty member at Oral Roberts University
I have considered these issues. The Oral Roberts Ministries is based
on the support of individual "partners." These are solicited through
direct mail appeals, the regular television programs of Oral and
Richard Roberts, and seminars held on the ORU campus. Some
of the appeals to individuals have been so controversial that they
have attracted national media attention, such as Oral Roberts'
statement that God would "call him home" if he did not raise $8
million dollars for medical missions in one year.

As an attorney I have also worked with individual philanthropy.
Estate planning is an obvious area—helping to draft wills or assisting in the administration of an estate according to the desires
of the testator. Legal issues also arise concerning a person's contributions during his lifetime and the various income-producing
types of contributions.

RESUMÉ OF A BOARD MEMBER

DR. EUGENE L. SWEARINGEN

EDUCATION:	Public Schools	Perry, Oklahoma
	Undergraduate	Northern Oklahoma Junior College 1937-1939
		Oklahoma State University, 1941
		Bachelor of Science in Business
	Graduate	Oklahoma State University, 1948
		Master of Science in Economics
		Stanford University, 1955
		Doctor of Philosophy in Economics
	Postdoctoral Summer Studies	Harvard University, Williams College, Dartmouth College, University of California
	Honorary Degree	Doctor of Laws, Oklahoma Christian College

POSITIONS:

Field Scout Executive for Boy Scouts of America, Texarkana, Arkansas - Texas, 1941-1943
Served in both Atlantic and Pacific Theaters, U. S. Naval Officer, 1943-1946
Field Scout Executive for Boy Scouts of America, Perry, Oklahoma, 1946-1947
Oklahoma State University: 1948-1967

1948-1956	All ranks from Instructor through Professor of Economics
1957-1965	Dean of the College of Business
1964-1966	Vice President for Development
1964-1965	Vice President for Academic Affairs
1966-1967	Vice President for Business and Finance

President, The University of Tulsa, 1967-1968
President, National Bank of Tulsa, 1968
President and Chief Executive Officer, National Bank of Tulsa, 1969-1972
Chairman of the Board & Chief Executive Officer, National Bank of Tulsa, (now Bank of Oklahoma) 1973-1978
Chairman of the Executive Committee, 1978-1980
Consulting Economist 1980-Present

RESUMÉ OF A BOARD MEMBER (Continued)

Professor of Free Enterprise - ORU 1982-Present
Holder of the Chair of Free Enterprise - ORU 1982-Present

PUBLICATIONS: Editor of a case book on business policy now in its fourth edition; has published numerous articles.

MANAGEMENT CONSULTANT: Served extensively as a Management Consultant to business organizations and conducted Management Development Programs for many different companies. Is past President of the National Council for Small Business Management Development.

OTHER: Listed in:
WHO'S WHO IN THE WORLD
Who's Who in American Education
Social and Behavioral Sciences Section of American Men and Women
Who's Who in the South and Southwest
Who's Who in Finance and Industry
Who's Who in America
Who's Who in Banking
Who's Who Among Authors and Journalists
Personalities in the South
Men of Achievement
Dictionary of International Biography
Honors:
1969 Man of the Year Award, presented by Downtown Tulsa Unlimited
Business Hall of Fame, Oklahoma State University, inducted in 1970
Marketing Man of the Year Award for 1971, Tulsa Chapter, American Marketing Association
Oklahoma Hall of Fame, 1973
Silver Knight of Management Award given by National Management Association, Tulsa Chapter, 1975
Award of Special Recognition by Arts Commission of the City of Tulsa, 1975
Oklahoma State University Alumni Hall of Fame, 1978
Chairman, Tulsa Area United Way, 1978
Member, Oklahoma State Regents for Higher Education, 1977-86
Chairman and Member of the Board of Trustees of the Southwestern Graduate School Foundation, 1977-83, Chairman 1980-82.
Chairman, Executive Service Corps of Tulsa, 1986-87

3

Corporations

INTRODUCTION

There is no legal mandate for corporations to give their money to nonprofit organizations, but corporations give as much money to nonprofit organizations as foundations give. The profit-making world meets the nonprofit world through corporate contributions programs. Why does corporate philanthropy exist?

Philanthropy is what societies use to compensate for the indifference of the marketplace and the incompetence of the state. Philanthropy involves both voluntary acts of compassion and voluntary acts of community (Payton 1984:18–19). Western philanthropy's roots of compassion began with ancient Jews and Christians, whereas its roots of community began with the classical Greeks and Romans. Philanthropy is the meeting of religion and economics.

One rationale for corporate philanthropy is preservation of the free enterprise system. Another rationale is to better corporate public relations, both external and internal. The basis for either rationale is the profit incentive. Yet both rationales lead to acts of compassion and of community by corporations to benefit their consumers as well as their employees. These motivations appear greater than any tax incentive because few corporations give even a fraction of the contributions that tax laws allow them to give.

Corporate contributions programs interact with one another both cooperatively and competitively. There are a variety of models for contributions programs within corporate hierarchies. Yet for all of them, the "people give to people" dimension is important.

MOTIVATIONS FOR CORPORATE PHILANTHROPY

Corporations depend on their resources and their consumers for corporate profits. Yet there is a tension between the obligations corporate executives feel toward their consumer public and the obligations they feel toward their own corporate shareholders. After all, shareholders want to see dividends. Consumers want quality products, and increasingly consumers demand even more, thus encouraging various forms of social activism by corporations. Corporations must also please their own corporate employees.

Corporate contributions are a means for corporations to please all three constituencies: their shareholders, their consumers, and their employees. Some, such as Irving Kristol, have argued that corporations owe a duty to give money only to their shareholders and not to nonprofit organizations. Others such as Lawrence Wien, a New York City attorney and real estate executive with the nickname "the Lone Ranger of Corporate Philanthropy," hold the opposite view. Wien's strategy is to buy stock in large corporations and, as a shareholder at the corporation's annual meeting, to advocate for the corporation to give away more money to philanthropy.

Of course, corporations also try to please their consumers. Ralph Nader's consumer advocacy has forced corporate accountability regarding the quality, especially the safety, of corporate products. In the late sixties and early seventies, student protesters directed some of their anger at corporations. Corporations became the villain to pacifists because businesses represented the military industrial complex. Corporations became the villain to environmentalists because manufacturing and mining polluted the air and water. Corporate leaders had always been the villain to left-wing political activists because the executives personified capitalism. Thus, corporations have confronted the challenges of outright threats of violence or consumer boycotts. Also, corporations may have the threat of urban violence coercing them into philanthropy to maintain peace and thereby promote viable business climates (Payton 1984:25).

Employees are the third corporate constituency. Corporations now have young executives who may have been among the student protesters, and corporations will attempt to retain them by various forms of community activism, including philanthropy. Corporations must also recruit from among recent college graduates who have grown up aware of consumer, environmental, and employee relations issues. Employee recruitment depends on the quality of life in the cities where corporations do business. Therefore, corporations make contributions to improve the business climate of those communities.

Corporations must publicize their philanthropy to consumers and to their employees in order to derive any benefit. Often, corporate contributions programs work closely with corporate public relations departments. The type of contributions corporations make will be affected by the public relations potential. For example, the corporation may choose to fund primarily those programs with high visibility. When I worked at Pennzoil we made a $1 million gift to interferon research (three gifts over three years). That was a high-visibility gift that prompted national media coverage for other corporations. Another high-visibility project at Pennzoil was helping to sponsor a public television program about the restoration of the *Elissa*, a nineteenth-century sailing ship. Public television specials are popular, high-visibility corporate contributions projects.

In contrast, corporations may be reluctant to sponsor new or controversial organizations that might cause negative publicity. A drug program in Houston received negative national television coverage. Several corporations' contributions officers met together and viewed a videotape of the negative publicity and discussed it before they made their decision about whether to donate to the drug program.

Corporations can publicize their philanthropy to their employees through internal corporate publications. At Pennzoil we regularly submitted to Pennzoil's internal publication, *Pennzoil Perspectives* material such as the following:

NATIONAL MERIT SCHOLARS HONORED

Four National Merit Scholarships have been awarded this year by Pennzoil. Three scholarships went to dependents of employees, and a one-time nonrenewable scholarship went to a fourth winner.

According to the National Merit Scholarship Corporation, the awards are "in recognition of outstanding performance and promise of future intellectual achievement." The winners . . . are Rebecca A. Fluharty (daughter of Charles J. Fluharty, head roustabout in Wallace, WVA), Solace H. Kirkland (daughter of John D. Kirkland, former Executive Vice President, in Houston), and Geoffrey F. Spradley (son of Jacqueline Spradley, Supervisor, Forms Management, in Houston). Karen K. Kozik of Malvern, PA, received a one-time scholarship.

As many as four National Merit Scholarships are made available to Pennzoil each year. However, all four scholarships are not necessarily awarded, depending on how many Pennzoil dependents qualify. Winners may receive from a minimum of $500 to a maximum of $1,500 per year of their college education. The National Merit Scholarship Committee chooses among children of Pennzoil employees on the basis of the results of their Preliminary Scholastic Aptitude Test/National Merit Scholarship Qualifying Test (PSAT/NMSQT), their academic record, leadership ability and significant extracurricular accomplishments.

. . . Those eligible for Pennzoil sponsored scholarships must be sons and daughters of regular Pennzoil employees, including children of domestic personnel of all subsidiaries, as well as children of retired and deceased employees. . . .

The . . . winners will be chosen from among the Pennzoil employee dependents who qualify as semifinalists. . . . The semifinalists will be sent applications to identify their parents' employers. These students should enter "Pennzoil Company" and the name of the division in which their parents work. Finalists will be selected without regard to financial need (*Pennzoil Perspectives* 1979:14).

Another Pennzoil contributions project that benefited employees was the Pennzoil sponsorship of employees' children's participation in the Amigos de las Americas program, a program that sends teens to live in villages in Latin America to give immunizations. We printed a brochure to let employees know the opportunity was available to their children.

Corporations will usually seek to give contributions to those organizations where their employees volunteer. Some allow their employees release time to do the volunteering. Corporations may also have "loaned executive" programs in which they loan one of their employees full-time to work for an agency. There is a problem, though, in how to hold the loaned employees' jobs for them until they return to the corporation. In Detroit the Accounting Aid Society is a combined corporate effort to loan the services of accountants to nonprofit organizations. Many corporations send executives to public schools to volunteer. In Houston, Tenneco sends thirty tutors a week to a Hispanic high school. It also provides landscaping of the grounds and takes the faculty on a summer retreat. Houston Lighting and Power sends professionals to teach units in their areas of expertise. *U.S. News and World Report* volunteers conduct workshops twice a week at a nearby junior high to help students enjoy writing. In Tulsa the AMOCO research center offers an enrichment course called "The Young Scientist." Company volunteers also demonstrate experiments in classrooms, and AMOCO opens its research lab on Saturday mornings for additional instruction for sixty of the brightest students.

Corporations will also make contributions to organizations that have served their employees. At Pennzoil we contributed to an agency that had helped an employee's child fight a drug problem. Of course, there must be confidentiality by the contributions department regarding contributions to agencies that have helped employees through sensitive difficulties such as alcohol, drugs, or interpersonal problems.

Matching gifts are another type of contribution where corporations seek to better their employee relations. The corporation may match employee gifts at a ratio of one-to-one or more. Most corporations make matching gifts to colleges and universities, and the Council for the Advancement and Support of Education (CASE) prints a brochure listing all corporations with matching gift programs for education. Corporations may also have matching gift programs for cultural and social service agencies. At Pennzoil we conducted a telephone survey of other corporate matching gifts programs before expanding into areas other than education.

For matching gifts programs, an employee makes a gift to his alma mater. Then either he or his alma mater contact the corporate contributions officer. In order to make the matching gift, the officer will need to know the employee name to verify he is an employee, and will need to know the size of the gift in order to match it with a corporate contribution. Employees who want their alma maters to receive matching gifts should have no problem with this disclosure requirement. Some corporations may put a ceiling on the size of gift they will match. Also, if a director or an employee makes a gift of corporate stock, there will need to be a procedure for matching it. The Conference Board reported that in 1984, securities were only 1% of corporate contributions, primarily from banking and insurance, with a median gift valued at approximately $500,000 (The Conference Board 1986:4).

Corporations want to maintain good employee relations, and corporate contributions can be used to better employee morale. Early railroad corporations were the forerunners of employee relations contributions programs, giving money to provide YMCA housing for railroad workers. Contributions can also be used to help instill a sense of camaraderie and community. At Pennzoil, employees received Pennzoil T-shirts to wear in a March of Dimes fund raiser described in a *Pennzoil Perspectives* article:

PENNZOIL JOINS MARCH OF DIMES SUPERWALK

Over 65 employees and their families donned yellow Pennzoil Company T-shirts to participate in Houston's March of Dimes Superwalk, March 23. Despite steady rain, many of the company's participants completed the full 35 kilometers (21 miles). As part of its contributions and community relations program, Pennzoil sponsored the employees and their immediate families at the rate of $1/kilometer.

Steve Veatch, planning analyst for Pennzoil Products, chose to *run* the full distance, crossing the finish line in first place. His time was 2 hours 18 minutes. Maureen, Kathryn, and Margaret Sullivan, daughters of Pennzoil hangar security guard Tom Sullivan, also elected to run and were the first females across the finish line. Their time was 3 hours and 22 minutes. It might have been faster, but they got lost and ran four extra miles. Several other Pennzoil parents had teenagers in the Superwalk.

Rock star Leif Garret and Houston Oiler Cheerleaders, the Derrick Dolls, were there to entertain the Superwalk crowds, which numbered nearly 10,000. There were rest stops and refreshments along the routes, as well as police guards and onlookers to encourage the Superwalkers.

The company hopes to offer other opportunities for employees and their families to get involved in community activities. Suggestions for future events are welcome and may be referred to the Contributions and Community Relations Department Manager Carla Weaver (*Pennzoil Perspectives* 1980:3).

There is some irony in the openness that corporations have toward interaction with the public through corporate contributions because some corporations have tight security to prevent outsiders from coming to their offices. In the Pennzoil building in Houston a fired employee of another company held its executives hostage. As a result Pennzoil tightened security with specialized computer card access to each floor. Mining companies typically have some of the tightest security, but most large corporations have some sort of security system. Employee badges are common. Corporate contributions programs can counter the depersonalization and isolation that such security causes by encouraging employee interaction with the community.

Since 1935, the tax laws have allowed deductions for corporate contributions. The current law allows corporations to give up to 10% of their pretax net income to nonprofit organizations. Despite the tax deduction incentive, many corporations give less than .5%. The Dayton Hudson Corporation in Minneapolis is a leader in encouraging corporations to give more toward the full percent allowed. E. B. Knauft, executive vice president of the Independent Sector, researched various corporate giving programs. He concluded that the most sophisticated contributions approach involves a target of contributions as a certain percentage of pretax corporate profits, based on the earnings of the past year or an average of the prior three years (Knauft 1985:4).

Another motivation for corporate contributions is political. Most corporate decision makers are politically conservative, favoring decentralized government with minimum restrictions on corporate activities. Their corporate contributions will be directed toward funding politically conservative organizations. Thus they support public policy organizations and many "free enterprise" programs. They may also refuse to contribute to universities that hire faculty with more liberal or left-wing political philosophies. Also, in order to reduce the power and budget of "big government," politically conservative corporations may give to social service programs themselves.

Corporations will also fund educational programs in fields related to their product. For example, energy companies will fund engineering education. Typically, corporate executives and directors will sponsor contributions to their own alma maters as well.

The motivations for corporate contributions—public relations, employee relations, tax incentives, preservation of the conservative social and political status quo, and educational affiliation—begin to explain the allocation of corporate contributions dollars. The interpersonal factor, "people give to people," is also important, and corporate executives support their own pet projects, influenced by such factors as friendships, status, and competition. In the male-dominated world of corporate executives, there is also the influence of their wives who encourage sponsorship of pet projects by their husbands' corporations.

Corporations compare their contributions to other corporations' contributions. In Houston, corporate contributions officers meet monthly to discuss their corporate giving. The Better Business Bureau organizes these luncheon meetings of the "Houston Group." No fund raisers are allowed to attend. The Better Business Bureau circulates a packet among all the members of the Houston Group before the meeting. The packet lists all the nonprofit organizations that have solicited any members and asks each member's response to the solicitation, including the actual amount given if any. At the luncheon meeting the results are available for all of the members. Thus, energy companies can learn what other energy companies have contributed to the same organizations. There is open formal discussion at the luncheon meeting. It serves, therefore, as a form of peer support for the contributions officers and helps to alleviate any "burnout." Yet there are ethical issues, such as whether the open discussion should include derogatory personal comments about any fund raiser. A nonprofit organization may lose corporate contributions if there has been a negative interaction with any corporate contributions officer who mentions it to his peers. In other cities, although there may be no formal meetings of corporate contributions officers, there may be informal networks. For example, the contributions officers may telephone one another to learn what each has done regarding a particular request. Such exchanges may include comments about the personal attributes of the fund raiser.

The Conference Board offers corporations the opportunity to

compare their contributions programs with other corporate contributions programs nationwide. Founded in 1916, the Conference Board is a nonprofit business information service whose purpose is to assist business leaders in their decision-making. The Conference Board has a staff of 350, with offices in New York City, Ottawa, and Brussels. It conducts international research and meetings, and it has associates in more than thirty-six hundred organizations and over fifty nations. It also conducts an annual survey of corporate contributions and publishes the results. Every fourth year it conducts an extremely detailed study.

Highlights of the 1984 study included growth in corporate giving as compared to the previous year: 1984 contributions were 26% higher than 1983 for U.S. corporations in the survey, whereas worldwide pretax income rose 13%. In comparison, IRS data showed an increase of 15% in U.S. corporate contributions, with worldwide pretax income rising 16%. Another highlight of the 1984 survey was that 1984 noncash giving of securities, company product, and property equipment together rose from 11% to 22% of total contributions. Gifts of property and equipment tripled, gifts of company product were two-and-a-half times greater, and gifts of securities doubled. Noncash gifts did not substitute for cash gifts, though. Cash gifts grew about 13%, at about the same rate as pretax profits. Another highlight of the 1984 Conference Board survey was that there was a dramatic increase in corporate assistance activities, the activities that do not qualify as federal tax deductions such as loaned executive programs, loans, deposits or investments at below-market yield, and the direct costs of administering the contributions program. Twenty-five percent more companies reported such activities than in 1983, and the amount they reported in 1984 was 76% greater than in 1983. The companies that reported in both years reported an 89% increase in the amount. The Conference Board survey also revealed a significant shift in the type of beneficiaries receiving corporate contributions, toward civic and community beneficiaries and away from health and human services. Gifts to education and to art and culture remained stable. Gifts to religious groups, groups that provide overseas aid, and miscellaneous programs decreased, as did United Way giving, as a proportion of all corporate contributions (The Conference Board 1986:v).

However, between 1984 and 1985, corporate contributions rose only 7%, to a fifteen-year high of $4.4 billion. For 1986, contributions were about 2.5% lower than in 1985. Oil companies cut back gifts by 15%. Other industries—chemicals, fabricated metals, nonelectric, and machinery—also had cutbacks. Mergers and acquisitions caused part of the change because one new company cannot give as much as its two parent companies were giving (*Fund Raising Management* 1987e:13). Food, banking, finance, pharmaceuticals, and autos are giving more. Also, more companies are linking contributions to corporate sales. They are also decentralizing contributions activities.

CORPORATE HIERARCHIES

Corporate contributions issues include the total level of giving, priorities and guidelines, and the internal and external environments of the corporation. E. B. Knauft's study included forty-eight corporate giving programs whose 1983 contributions ranged from .6% to 5% of pretax income, with a mean of 1.9%. There were thirty manufacturing and eighteen nonmanufacturing companies in fifteen different industry classifications. Of those companies, 77% had a corporate foundation. The corporate foundation model includes a foundation staff, an intermediate level of management for foundation officers, and with the CEO (Chief Executive Officer) for a foundation officer, and the foundation Board of Trustees. The foundation's funding comes from the corporation (Knauft 1985:7).

In contrast, the corporate contribution program model begins with field committees, who report to a contributions staff, who report to an intermediate level of management. Next there is a contributions committee, followed by the CEO and the Corporate Board of Directors and its board committees. Frequently there are both corporate contributions programs and corporate foundations in the same company, and the same individuals serve on the boards or staffs. The key individuals, however, are the CEO and the manager of the contributions staff. Knauft found that the internal committees vary, but most are capable assistants to the contributions staffs. The staffs in the study ranged in size from one to twenty professional staff, with a median of three, and from one to twenty-six administrative staff, with a median of two. The internal committee members are usually upper- and middle-level line and staff managers, but several companies, especially the smaller ones, include rank-and-file employees on their committees (Knauft 1985:7).

The role of the CEO is crucial to a successful corporate contributions program. The CEO is the advocate from the contributions staff and committees to the corporate Board of Directors. He may attempt to influence the contributions program more than outside board members will. Yet in some companies the CEO may arbitrarily exert his authority to justify contributions to his own pet projects, ignoring the priorities and recommendations established by the contributions staff. Some companies attempt to counteract this tendency by setting aside a certain amount in the contributions budget as discretionary funds for senior management, or by using operating funds from the CEO's own cost center, or simply by having the CEO make such contributions out of his own personal funds.

The Knauft study identified models of behavior of the contributions manager, of whom 52% were male and 48% were female. One type of manager is the "loyal soldier" who receives orders from the CEO and dutifully obeys, while committees and boards perfunctorily rubber-stamp grant recommendations. Another type of manager is the "skillful tactician" who has a loyalty to the CEO and who works with a constituency of company managers who have high credibility with the CEO. This contributions manager generally supports whatever he believes the committees or foundation boards will approve. Another type of contributions manager is the "change agent" who works to change either the content of corporate contributions or the process whereby the corporation decides what grants to make. A change agent may create change in content by first creating change in the process, working toward candid discussions that resolve in consensus about the content of contributions. Another type of contributions manager is the "broker-advocate" who works for his own pet project in the community, but who needs to be wary of alienating the upper corporate hierarchy in the process. The final type of contributions manager is the "technocrat" who runs contributions strictly by the priority rules he has established himself. Most managers are a combination of these types (Knauft 1985:13).

People give to people in corporations. A nonprofit organization should survey its board members and its other fund raisers regarding who knows CEOs and who has a relationship to CEOs conducive to soliciting funds from them. The organization should also review the remaining corporate hierarchy of presidents, vice presidents, and other corporate executives, including the contributions manager, to determine which board members might know those individuals. The officers' names will be in the corporation's annual report.

When I worked at Pennzoil there was a Contributions Committee of top executives who circulated a voting sheet about contributions among themselves. They often added their own comments and attachments to the sheet to persuade or dissuade the others. A majority vote meant the corporation would make the contribution.

As a contributions analyst, I screened initial proposal letters. We discouraged telephone solicitations. My screeing consisted of determining whether the proposal fit any of Pennzoil's rationales for corporate contributions. If not, we sent a form "no" letter to the organization, and we maintained a file of those organizations we rejected. Eventually that information was computerized.

I also met with fund raisers in person. If the person was a Pennzoil employee, he had a better chance of securing funding for his project. If we met as strangers, with no Pennzoil connections, then we had to deal with the interpersonal dimension immediately. It was at that point that a project's funding could be won or lost. Subconsciously I would note my first impressions of the person. How was he dressed? Most corporations have a "dress for success" dress code. At Pennzoil it was possible to tell a person's position by his dress: mailboys wore blue jeans, executives wore suits and ties, etc. I know of one corporate contributions officer in Colorado who was solicited for a contribution by a woman wearing a traditional Native American costume. The corporate contributions officer had scheduled a luncheon with the woman in the corporate executive dining room. Yet, when she saw her guest's costume, she decided it would be inappropriate and awkward to take her there. Some may argue that the fund raiser's costume was a necessary part of her social statement. Perhaps. The contributions officer was concerned that other executives in the dining room would have guests for business deals and might be embarrassed. The interpersonal relationship was harmed, and a contribution was jeopardized as a result.

Besides first impressions, the meeting with a corporate contributions officer will include other "people give to people" aspects. Does the fund raiser appear confident? Psychological factors are at work, factors such as transference, where I perceive the fund raiser to have qualities of someone else I know, and projection, where I amplify characteristics of the fund raiser that remind me of myself. Timing is also a factor. For example, if the interview is right before lunch, everyone may be preoccupied with hunger. Some fund raisers avoid Monday appointments and Friday afternoons in deference to the corporate executive's schedule. At Pennzoil I was often the luncheon guest of fund raisers. This was a pleasant way of sampling Houston restaurants, but there is a point where contributions officer "burnout" may occur. Some contributions officers may even prefer a sack lunch alone to the experience of luncheon solicitations. Generally, the requests for money will come during dessert. This may be awkward, especially if either party feels rushed.

The corporate contributions officer also faces the danger of feeling guilty about saying no. There simply may be a greater number of worthwhile causes than the current contributions budget can support. The officer may have a strategy for increasing the next year's budget, but in the meantime some projects can't be funded. The fund raiser should know in advance the corporation's deadline for proposals for that year's budget. The contributions officer will need to be secure enough in his role to say no graciously, without undermining the corporation. Ideally, the contributions officer will feel comfortable suggesting other funding sources to the fund raiser and the fund raiser will be open to suggestions. The fund raiser may need to rewrite the proposal, with more charts and statistics and less verbiage, to appeal to corporate businessmen.

THE IDEAL CORPORATE CONTRIBUTIONS PROGRAM

There is no publication that attempts to rank corporate contributions programs, such as Waldemar Nielsen's *The Golden Donors* does for foundations. Corporate contributions programs, even with corporate foundations, are newer than general foundation programs. Corporate contributions began as a method of improving the public image of corporations. There are, though, surveys of corporate contributions programs conducted by the Conference Board, the Independent Sector, the Council on Foundations, and others. There is even a *National Directory of Corporate Charity* published by the Foundation Center.

An ideal corporate giving program has several characteristics. One is that there must be commitment to the program by the chief executive officer. He should strive for a competitive contributions program. There should be a discretionary category in the budget of approximately 20% (Knauft 1985:9).

It is difficult to determine whether or not having a corporate foundation necessarily affects the quality of the contributions program. The incentives for having a foundation include the possibility of the corporation, as well as its principal shareholders, directors, and anyone else, making contributions to the company foundation. Most corporate foundations, unlike private independent foundations, do not depend on their endowment income to make grants because they receive money from the sponsoring corporation. Yet, an endowment income can be accumulated. In 1985, corporate foundations probably earned at least $200 million in endowment income (White 1987:1). Assets in corporate foundations also provide a cushion for corporate contributions in years when the corporation has lower profits. In addition, establishment of a corporate foundation helps the corporation to conceptualize its contributions policies.

The ideal corporate contributions program should have a formal mechanism for input from a variety of types of employees, including management and rank-and-file employees. Employee volunteerism should be recognized as a part of the contributions program, with cash grants made according to employee interests. Employee release time and loaned executive time should be included as noncash dimensions of contributions budget targets. The budgets for each corporate location should reflect the number of employees there and their interests. There should be targeted amounts for cash contributions and in-kind gifts even if there is no targeting of a percentage of pretax profits.

Management of the program should operate according to the same styles as the rest of the corporation. If other corporate divisions work by management by objectives, the contributions area should do so too. The mission of the program should be identified as to how the program serves both corporate and community interests. Areas of giving should be prioritized according to the overall mission. Knauft suggests that no more than 10 to 15% of the grants be exceptions to the prioritized guidelines. The priorities should be reassessed routinely; Knauft suggests every three years (Knauft 1985:9).

The corporation needs to publicize specific information about its program, including the targeted amount for the contributions budget in future years, its funding priorities, the procedure for grant applications, and previous grant recipients and the amount they received. This information should be made available to all employees and to the communities where the corporation does business. There should be publicity mailings to former grant recipients, special interest groups, elected officials, media representatives, and other corporate and foundation grantmakers. The corporation should also publicize its contributions program through publications such as the *National Directory of Corporate Charity*.

Once the corporation establishes priorities, it should hire a manager and staff for the contributions department. They should have expertise and interest in the prioritized areas or a willingness to seek out experts. There should be candid analysis of what role the contributions manager will play in relation to the CEO, other managers, board members, and the community, with the CEO helping to write the job description.

Record keeping should be as careful and efficient as in other corporate departments. Preferably it should be computerized. All funding requests, as well as the corporate response, should be recorded. The corporation's reply to each request should be timely. Knauft suggests the corporation reply within three months (Knauft 1985:9).

The corporation also needs to reach an agreement with grant recipients about methods of evaluation. There should be at least one site visit to each recipient. Repetitive grants should be routinely reassessed.

EFFECTS OF THE 1986 TAX ACT

The magnitude of the impact of the 1986 tax law on corporate contributions is uncertain. The maximum corporate tax rate dropped from 46% to 34%, meaning that where corporations formerly saved 46 cents for every dollar given to charity, they now save only 34 cents per dollar. It is uncertain how the new tax provisions will be factored into corporate budgets (*Fund Raising Management* 1987e:13).

Similar to individual gifts, corporate gifts of appreciated property to nonprofit charities may be more costly if the corporation is subject to the alternative minimum tax. Also, except for gifts of publicly traded stock, the deduction for all gifts of appreciated property given to the corporate foundation are limited to the corporation's cost or basis in the property.

The 1986 law requires corporate foundations and all private foundations to pay their excise tax on investment income quarterly rather than on the date their Form 990-PF tax return is filed. Deposits should not be made to the IRS but to qualified bank depositories. The 1986 law also allows corporations to donate new tangible scientific property of an inventory nature not only to colleges and universities, as before, but also to nonprofit organizations founded and operated primarily to do scientific research. Also, corporations may deduct all the cost of attending a sporting event if the event is organized primarily to benefit a charity, with 100% of its net proceeds going to charity, and if it uses volunteers for all the work on the event.

PERSONAL EXPERIENCES

I was a personal friend of Pennzoil's manager of contributions and community relations, Carla Weaver, before I went to work there. We created the position of "contributions analyst" together, selecting the job title in preference to more vague titles, such as "research assistant." I assisted Carla in the initial review of grant applications. I also helped facilitate the conceptualization of contributions policy toward social service organizations; I enjoyed bringing a social worker perspective to the corporate environment. In addition, I helped coordinate Pennzoil employee participation in community activities.

When I worked at Pennzoil, my father was vice president of acquisitions for American Petrofina. Although he has been a corporate oil man his entire career, becoming an "independent" only recently, I went to work at Pennzoil with very little insight into corporate life. I came from the nonprofit sector with a somewhat self-righteous attitude toward corporations.

My first impressions at Pennzoil were of the similarity of corporate life to what I imagined military life to be. For instance, it was important for everyone to be "in uniform." On one of my first days at Pennzoil, a secretary friend and I tried to go from our twenty-ninth floor office to see the office of the CEO, Hugh Liedtke, about six floors up. Neither of us was dressed like a professional. As we were getting off the elevator at the CEO's floor, a security guard suddenly appeared and told us it was forbidden for us to be there. He took my friend's name and sent us back to our offices. On another day, when the CEO was out of town, I was dressed like a professional as I accompanied the manager of contributions and community relations not only to look at the impressive mineral collection just outside the CEO's office but also to watch "The Donahue Show" on the television inside his office suite. Otherwise, I had no contact with Hugh Liedtke except when we occasionally rode the elevator together in the mornings. It seemed to me that the president, Baine Kerr, took a more active role regarding corporate contributions.

My friend, Carla Weaver, the manager of contributions, had her MBA degree. She had been transferred from Pennzoil's corporate planning department after it had been dismantled. Robert Payton provides an accurate portrayal of the short career ladders of corporate contributions officers. Promotion may mean moving back into the corporate mainstream, out of contributions (Payton 1984:84). Carla was the first person to actually formalize Pennzoil's contributions program. She helped establish target contributions amounts. She also challenged the executives on Pennzoil's Contributions Committee to reassess whether large contributions to the alma mater of one of the directors were appropriate when that university did not offer any degree related to energy, mining, or Pennzoil's business. Pennzoil supported politically conservative organizations, but there are legal restrictions on corporate political activities. Therefore, Carla had to decline an outside invitation to work in George Bush's 1980 attempt at the presidential nomination. George Bush and Hugh Liedtke had been in the oil business together in West Texas years before.

Our office was responsible for overseeing Pennzoil's nationwide contributions budget of approximately $1.5 million. We were part of Pennzoil's Public Relations Department. The following are sample memos from my work:

TO: Carla Weaver
FROM: Lynda Adams
RE: Houston Museum of Natural Science

Summarizing my telephone conversation before our visit with Dr. Pulley, the Director of the Houston Museum of Natural Science:

—The Museum has not applied to the American Association of Museums' accreditation program because they feel it is not up to the calibre of similar accreditation programs for universities, hospitals, etc.

—The Museum is the second largest science museum in Texas, the largest being in Ft. Worth.

—Nationally, the Museum is in the medium-size category, while the largest include the most famous: Smithsonian American Museum, Field Museum in Chicago, California Museum of Natural Science, Denver, and Cleveland Museums.

—Dr. Pulley feels that the Museum's relative newness (it is only ten years old), accounts for its relative size.

—There are approximately 600,000 visitors to the Museum each year, but the Peruvian Gold Show brought an additional 200,000.

—The Hall of Petroleum Science and Technology began with a grant from the Harry C. Wiess foundation from the man who was the founder of Humble Oil Company. The $630,000 request for the Hall will be used to provide income used toward the operating costs of the Hall such as utility bills.

TO: Carla Weaver
FROM: Lynda Adams
RE: Inter-Tribal Council

   On November 16 I met with Susan Smith of the Inter-Tribal Council
and Dr. Ronald Rea who is a city-appointed consultant to the project.
(He was a speaker at the "Meeting of the Minds" Seminar.) The organization is in the infant stage. They only recently received their 501(c)(3)
status. Their staff consists of a volunteer Director and 1–3 C.E.T.A.
placements. (Susan Smith is one.) There is an elected Board of Directors with nine members and two alternates which had been meeting
weekly.
   In our meeting I learned the history of the organization, e.g. it has been
unsuccessful in obtaining federal funding, probably due to lack of experience in dealing with the bureaucracy. I suggested they review research
on the Indian population by U. of H., the School of Public Health, etc.
(The Alabama Coushatta and Tigua are the main local tribes.) The Council is also in competition with Dallas for state funds because the B.I.A.
relocation project was directed at Dallas, and therefore, Houston could
not prove as great a need. They have received $5,000 from Gulf Coast
Community Services and $2,500 from the Campaign for Human Devel-
opment. I offered suggestions for their approach to corporations and reviewed other sources of support with them.

TO: Dave Smith
FROM: Lynda Adams
cc: Carla Weaver
RE: Noteworthy Contributions

   Pennzoil contributions . . . included gifts to educational, civic, and cultural institutions throughout the nation. Pennzoil Company gave $2,500
to Victoria Junior College for the Handicapped. This Texas institution
provides encouragement to handicapped students who may then continue
their college education at 4-year campuses. We also gave $2,750 to help
sponsor Princeton's "Business Today Seminar" in which Pennzoil sent
three employees to meet with other professionals and a select group of
college students from across the nation. Their topic was the business outlook for the 80's. In addition, we gave $10,000 to the American Heart
Association. Pennzoil in Houston also gave $1,000 to the High School
for Engineering Professions. We have one PBS program in progress and
others under consideration. This year Pennzoil expanded its matching
corporate gifts program to include the United Way campaigns at all Pennzoil locations.

TO: Carla Weaver
FROM: Lynda Adams
RE: AWARE Dinner

The 16 women from Pennzoil sat at the two tables nearest the Speakers Table. Not only did that give us "ringside seats," but we were also spotlighted on the Channel 11 news story about the dinner on the 10:00 news. Overall, the group's response was favorable toward the evening. It was a get acquainted time for many of the women who had never met each other during their regular work reponsibilities.

The Speakers were good. Rose Klimist, the AWARE Coordinator for this area, gave a brief welcome, and Ben Adams, Chairman on Energy for the NAACP of Texas, gave the Invocation (Psalms 23). Louie Welch was not present to give the opening remarks, and the program continued with the Guest Speakers: 1) Lt. Governor Bill Hobby, who warned of the Soviet threat in the strategic Strait of Harmuz and encouraged greater domestic production, friendliness toward Arabs enrolled in U.S. colleges, use of synthetic fuels, and investment in energy reserves in China; 2) Assistant Director of NASA, Bob Pyland, who gave a slide presentation about satellite use in solar energy development; 3) Miles Reynolds, an Engineer from Coastal States Gas, who apologized for his "engineer jargon" to the audience which was 1/3 men, and then discussed the economics of the world oil situation and encouraged nuclear stimulation to release impermeable natural gas; 4) Dr. David Lamkin of Los Alamos Scientific Laboratory who gave a slide presentation to describe the use of nuclear power and then discussed the issues of a) reactor safety, b) nuclear waste disposal, c) environmental impact, and d) fears of the proliferation of nuclear weaponry; and 5) League of Women Voters representatives Laura Keever, who explained that the League's position is very cautious toward the development of nuclear reactors but that they encourage the sound use of coal resources, among others, and she urged the audience to impact energy policy by contacting a) the Texas Railroad Commission, b) the Texas Utility Commission, c) the Texas Department of Health Radiation Control branch, and d) the Texas Energy and Natural Resources Council.

Attached is the program from the Dinner and a sample participant response.

My most recent experience with corporate contributions has been my guest speakers from corporations in my "Successful Fund Raising" class:

Forrest Brokaw—Sun Company
Clyde Cole—President, Tulsa Chamber of Commerce

Leonard Eaton—Chief Executive Officer and Chairman of the Board, Bank of Oklahoma, Tulsa

Lewis J. Fitzgerald—Director, Corporate Communications, Reading & Bates Corp.

E. Booth Moffit, Jr.—Vice President, Public Service Co., Tulsa

Ruth Munsch—Executive Manager, Phillips Petroleum Foundation, Inc., and Corporate Contribution Analyst, Phillips, Bartlesville, Oklahoma

Dr. John Piercey—Director, Department of City Development, Office of the Mayor, Tulsa

Pierce Reynolds—"Loaned Executive" to Moton Clinic by Sun Company.

JOB DESCRIPTION AND PROFILE OF A CORPORATE CONTRIBUTIONS EXECUTIVE: C. FORREST BROKAW, JR., SUN COMPANY

Contributions and Community Relations Job Description

1. Administer local area contributions budget of $100,000 to $200,000 through chairmanship of a Contributions Sub-Committee and as secretary of top-level management group that constitutes the Contributions Committee. The Sub-Committee is a sort of "working" group which makes site visits and spends more time on the requests than do the members of the management group. All requests for funds, whether classified as IRS-designated charitable organizations, community relations organizations, or business memberships, are processed, investigated, and evaluated through this department of one.

2. Guide, promote, and set targets for annual United Way campaign which most recently saw nearly $200,000 donated by employees, and a matching amount from the company.

3. Evaluate the need for, and recruit from the ranks of managers, representatives from the company to serve on major boards in the community—Boards ranging from Tulsa Council on Alcoholism and the Tulsa Psychiatric Center, to the YMCA, TJC, and the NCCJ.

4. Maintain a familiarity with community needs and activities so that evaluation of company involvements is targeted in the most advantageous ways. Involvements include contributions, board representation, and loaned executives. The company has a history of lending executives to community and civic organizations for periods of time ranging from three months to two years. The executives are sometimes "fast

track" young persons who need a change of pace. At times, the community need arises first, and we then search for the most appropriate loaned executive candidate. Sometimes we identify the executive and search for an appropriate task in the community. Three of the most recent loaned executives in Tulsa were (a) the former manager of our refinery who was loaned to Moton Health Center for eighteen months to raise capital funds and to aid in business processes, (b) the former manager of our refinery laboratory who was loaned to the Hazardous Materials Response Team of the City-County to help in training of personnel in handling hazardous material and in identifying the types of materials that could prove hazardous in Tulsa, and (c) the former manager of our Information Systems group in Tulsa who was loaned to the City of Tulsa for a two-year period beginning July 1, 1986, to work with the departments concerned with economic development.

5. Try to leverage all contributions, since the company's available dollars are not as many as some companies' and since our employee ranks are not as large as some. We do this by issuing challenge grants, funding specific "seed" projects, and coming up with truly unique leadership grants before anyone else acts on the need.

This overall task is the responsibility of the Public Relations Department, in addition to its regular internal and external communications tasks.

BIOGRAPHY—JANUARY 1985

C. Forrest Brokaw, Jr., is Tulsa area manager of Public Relations for Sun Company. He has been accredited by the Public Relations Society of America since 1982 for his demonstration of proficiency in Public Relations.

He is responsible for all internal and external communications programs and community relations activities for Sun Pipe Line Company from the Gulf of Mexico to the Great Lakes; from Midland, Texas, to Syracuse, New York. In addition, he is responsible for local public relations on behalf of the parent company and its other operating units in Tulsa, and he is the primary public contact for Sun in Tulsa.

Brokaw, who was loaned by Sun in 1979 to handle national promotion for the PBS program "Over Easy" in San Francisco and in 1980 to develop public relations programs for the American Productivity Center in Houston, was regional manager of Sun's Corporate Communications in Tulsa from 1976 to 1979. Previously he has served as reporter for KVOO Radio, 1951–1953; reporter for *Tulsa Tribune*, 1954; manager for KUSH radio in Cushing, 1955–1956; news director for KVOO radio and television combined, 1956–1961; news director for KELI radio, 1961–1972; and general manager for KIXZ radio in Amarillo, Texas, 1972–1974. He joined Sun in Dallas in 1975 as external public relations consultant.

Active in community affairs, he is a member of the following boards: Downtown Tulsa Unlimited, National Conference of Christians and Jews Tulsa Chapter, Society of Professional Journalists/Sigma Delta Chi, and the Tulsa Chapter of the Public Relations Society of America. He is a member of the administrative board of Christ United Methodist Church, the Public Relations Committee for the Oklahoma-Kansas Oil and Gas Association, Tulsa's Corporate Volunteer Council, the Oil Writers Association of America, and the Tulsa Press Club. He is a former president of the Tulsa Press Club, the Eastern Oklahoma Chapter of Sigma Delta Chi, the Professional Journalism Society, and the Tulsa Chapter of the Public Relations Society of America.

Brokaw has been in the public communications field since 1944 when he began working as KGFF radio in Shawnee, Oklahoma. He is a past winner of awards from the Oklahoma UPI Broadcasters, the state AP Broadcasters, the Pubic Relations Society of America, and the Oklahoma Petroleum Council.

4

Foundations

INTRODUCTION

There is a certain mystique about foundations. The largest ones were created by some of our nation's wealthiest men: Ford, Rockefeller, Carnegie. Foundations symbolize an American dream of financial success overflowing to reward the society that helped provide that success.

Because of the mystique surrounding foundations they also represent a potential danger for new fund raisers. The danger is that new fund raisers will have a "pie in the sky" attitude toward foundations. They may reason that all they need to do is research the foundations, find all the foundations interested in funding their type of project, and then, applying a scatter-gun approach, mail the same proposal to each of those foundations. This method is wrong because it fails to recognize that each foundation is unique. It fails to account for the fact that "people give to people" in foundations too. This method is also dangerous because it diverts fund raising energy and efforts away from individuals. Certain organizations, such as religious organizations, will have more difficulty in receiving any foundation funds. In fact, only about 2% of foundation gifts go to churches or religious organizations, compared to 70% of individual gifts. Also, although it is true that the large foundations are able to give very large gifts, with an average gift of $50,000 in 1982 compared to an average individual gift of $475, the competition for funds from the large foundations is great. The time spent cultivating a gift from a large foundation might be better spent cultivating twenty gifts from individuals who, unlike foundations, will be more likely to sustain or even increase their financial support in succeeding years. At any rate, current areas of interest among foundations are natural and human resources, communications, the service industry, ethics, international affairs, and social issues (Broce 1986:127).

SOURCES OF INFORMATION

Fund raising from foundations may seem much easier than fund raising from individuals and corporations because information about foundations is more accessible. Foundations are legal creations subject to federal and state regulations. By law, foundations must give away a certain percentage of their assets each year. IRS forms are obvious sources of information about foundation giving. The IRS forms 990–AR (Annual Report) and 990–PF (Private Foundations) provide information about foundation assets, annual contributions, officers, directors, trustees, and finances. This information is available on microfiche cards.

This easy access to foundation information came about largely because of congressional pressure to improve foundations' accountability to the public. Congressional probes of foundation activities have provided the impetus to some foundations to change from being paranoid enclaves to being more open with the public. The threat of actually abolishing foundations altogether has forced foundations to improve their public image (Edie 1985).

THE FOUNDATION CENTER

The Foundation Center in New York helps fund raisers obtain foundation information. After congressional investigations in 1950 James Perkins of the Carnegie Corporation and John Gardner started the Foundation Library Center. It became the Foundation Center after the famous 1969 congressional investigation known as the Patman hearings for Congressman Patman, who was a powerful critic of foundations. The center helps maintain 150 reference collections.

Reference Collections Operated by the Foundation Center

The Foundation Center
79 Fifth Avenue
New York, NY 10003
212-620-4230

The Foundation Center
1001 Connecticut Avenue, N.W.
Washington, DC 20036
202-331-1400

The Foundation Center
Kent H. Smith Library

1442 Hanna Building
1422 Euclid Avenue
Cleveland, OH 44115
216-861-1933

The Foundation Center
312 Sutter Street
San Francisco, CA 94108
415-397-0902

Cooperating Collections

ALABAMA

Birmingham Public Library
2020 Park Place
Birmingham 35203
205-226-3600

Huntsville-Madison County Public
   Library
108 Fountain Circle
P.O. Box 443
Huntsville, 35804
205-536-0021

Auburn University at Montgomery
   Library
Montgomery 36193-0401
205-279-9649

ALASKA

University of Alaska, Anchorage
   Library
3211 Providence Drive
Anchorage 99508
907-786-1848

ARIZONA

Phoenix Public Library
Business and Sciences Department
12 E. McDowell Road
Phoenix 85004
602-262-4636

Tucson Public Library
Main Library
200 S. Sixth Avenue
Tucson 85701
602-791-4393

ARKANSAS

Westark Community College Library
Grand Avenue at Waldron Road
Fort Smith 72913
501-785-4241

Little Rock Public Library
Reference Department
700 Louisiana Street
Little Rock 72201
501-370-5950

CALIFORNIA

California Community Foundation
Funding Information Center
3580 Wilshire Boulevard, Suite 1660
Los Angeles 90010
213-413-4042

Community Foundation for Monterey County
420 Pacific Street
Monterey 93940
408-375-9712

California Community Foundation
4050 Metropolitan Drive #300
Orange 92668
714-937-9077

Riverside Public Library
3581 Seventh Street
Riverside 92501
714-787-7201

California State Library
Reference Services, Rm. 309
914 Capital Mall
Sacramento 95814
916-322-4570

San Diego Community Foundation
625 Broadway, Suite 1015
San Diego 92101
619-239-8815

Grantsmanship Resource Center
Junior League of San Jose, Inc.
Community Foundation of Santa Clara County

960 West Hedding, Suite 220
San Jose 95126
408-244-5280

Orange County Community Development Council
1440 E. First Street, 4th Floor
Santa Ana 92701
714-547-6801

Peninsula Community Foundation
1204 Burlingame Avenue
Burlingame 94011-0627
415-342-2505

Santa Barbara Public Library
Reference Section
40 East Anapamu
P.O. Box 1019
Santa Barbara 93102
805-962-7653

Santa Monica Public Library
1343 Sixth Street
Santa Monica 90401-1603
213-458-8603

Tuolomne County Library
465 S. Washington Street
Sonora 95370
209-533-5707

COLORADO

Pikes Peak Library District
20 N. Cascade Avenue
Colorado Springs 80901
303-473-2080

Denver Public Library
Sociology Division
1357 Broadway
Denver 80203
303-571-2190

CONNECTICUT

Danbury Public Library
155 Deer Hill Avenue
Danbury 06810
203-797-4505

Hartford Public Library
Reference Department
500 Main Street
Hartford 06103
203-525-9121

D.A.T.A.
880 Asylum Avenue
Hartford 06105
203-278-2477

D.A.T.A.
25 Science Park, Suite 502
New Haven 06513
203-786-5225

DELAWARE

Hugh Morris Library
University of Delaware
Newark 19717-5267
302-451-2965

FLORIDA

Volusia County Public Library
City Island
Daytona Beach 32014
904-252-8374

Jacksonville Public Library
Business, Science, and Industry Department
122 N. Ocean Street
Jacksonville 32202
904-633-3926

Miami-Dade Public Library
Humanities Department
101 W. Flagler Street

Miami 33132
305-375-2665

Orlando Public Library
10 N. Rosalind
Orlando 32801
305-425-4694

University of West Florida
John C. Pace Library
Pensacola 32514
904-474-2412

Selby Public Library
1001 Boulevard of the Arts
Sarasota 33577
813-366-7303

Leon County Public Library
Community Funding Resources
   Center
1940 N. Monroe Street
Tallahassee 32303
904-478-2665

Palm Beach County Community
   Foundation
324 Datura Street, Suite 340
West Palm Beach 33401
305-659-6800

GEORGIA

Atlanta-Fulton Public Library
Ivan Allen Department
1 Margaret Mitchell Square
Atlanta 30303
404-688-4636

HAWAII

Thomas Hale Hamilton Library
University of Hawaii
General References
2550 The Mall

Honolulu 96822
808-948-7214

Community Resource Center
The Hawaiian Foundation
Financial Plaza of the Pacific
111 S. King Street
Honolulu 96813
808-525-8548

IDAHO

Caldwell Public Library
1010 Dearborn Street
Caldwell 83605
208-459-3242

ILLINOIS

Belleville Public Library
121 W. Washington Street
Belleville 62220
618-234-0441

DuPage Township
300 Briarcliff Road
Bolingbrook 60439
312-759-1317

Donors Forum of Chicago
53 W. Jackson Boulevard, Rm. 430
Chicago 60604
312-726-4882

Evanston Public Library
1703 Orrington Avenue
Evanston 60201
312-866-0305

Sangamon State University Library
Shepherd Road
Springfield 62708
217-786-6633

INDIANA

Allen County Public Library
900 Webster Street

Fort Wayne 46802
219-424-7241

Indiana University Northwest Library
3400 Broadway
Gary 46408
219-980-6580

Indianapolis—Marion County
  Public Library
40 E. St. Clair Street
Indianapolis 46204
317-269-1733

IOWA

Public Library of Des Moines
100 Locust Street
Des Moines 50309
505-283-4259

KANSAS

Topeka Public Library
Adult Services Department
1515 W. Tenth Street
Topeka 66604
913-233-2040

Wichita Public Library
223 S. Main
Wichita 67202
316-262-0611

KENTUCKY

Western Kentucky University
Division of Library Services
Helm-Cravens Library
Bowling Green 42101
502-745-3951

Louisville Free Public Library
Fourth and York Streets
Louisville 40203
503-223-7201

LOUISIANA

East Baton Rouge Parish Library
Centroplex Library
120 St. Louis Street
Baton Rouge 70821
504-389-4960

New Orleans Public Library
Business and Science Division
219 Loyola Avenue
New Orleans 70140
504-589-2583

Shreve Memorial Library
424 Texas Street
Shreveport 71101
318-226-5894

MAINE

University of Southern Main Center for Research and Advanced
Study
246 Deering Avenue
Portland 04102
207-780-4411

MARYLAND

Enoch Pratt Free Library
Social Science and History Department
400 Cathedral Street
Baltimore 21201
301-396-5320

MASSACHUSETTS

Associated Grantmakers of Massachusetts
294 Washington Street, Suite 501
Boston 02108
617-426-2608

Boston Public Library
Copley Square

Boston 02117
617-536-5400

Walpole Public Library
Common Street
Walpole 02081
617-668-5497, ext. 340

Western Massachusetts Funding
Resource Center
Campaign for Human Develop-
ment
Chancery Annex
73 Chestnut Street
Springfield 01103
413-732-3175, ext. 67

Grants Resource Center
Worcester Public Library
Salem Square
Worcester 01608
617-799-1655

MICHIGAN

Alpena County Library
211 N. First Avenue
Alpena 49707
517-356-6188

University of Michigan—Ann Arbor
Reference Department
209 Hatcher Graduate Library
Ann Arbor 48109-1205
313-764-1149

Henry Ford Centennial Library
16301 Michigan Avenue
Dearborn 48126
313-943-2337

Purdy Library
Wayne State University
Detroit 48202
313-577-4040

Michigan State University Libraries
Reference Library
East Lansing 48824
517-353-9184

Farmington Community Library
32737 W. Twelve Mile Road
Farmington Hills 48018
313-553-0300

University of Michigan—Flint
  Library
Reference Department
Flint 48503
313-762-3408

Grand Rapids Public Library
Sociology and Education Depart-
  ment
Library Plaza
Grand Rapids 49502
616-456-4411

Michigan Technological University
  Library
Highway U.S. 41
Houghton 49931
906-487-2507

MINNESOTA

Duluth Public Library
520 Superior Street
Duluth 55802
218-723-3802

Southwest State University Library
Marshall 56258
507-537-7278

Minneapolis Public Library
Sociology Department
300 Nicollet Mall
Minneapolis 55401
612-372-6555

Rochester Public Library
Broadway at First Street, S.E.
Rochester 55901
507-285-8002

Saint Paul Public Library
90 W. Fourth Street
Saint Paul 55102
612-292-6311

MISSISSIPPI

Jackson Metropolitan Library
301 N. State Street
Jackson 39201
601-944-1120

MISSOURI

Clearinghouse for Midcontinent
  Foundations
University of Missouri, Kansas City
P.O. Box 22680
Law School, Suite 1-300
Fifty-Second Street and Oak
Kansas City 64113
816-276-1176

Kansas City Public Library
311 E. Twelfth Street
Kansas City 64106
816-221-2685

Metropolitan Association for Philanthropy, Inc.
5585 Pershing Avenue, Suite 150
St. Louis 63112
314-361-3900

Springfield—Greene County Library
397 E. Central Street
Springfield 65801
417-866-4636

MONTANA

Eastern Montana College Library
Reference Department

1500 N. Thirtieth Street
Billings 59101-0298
406-657-2262

Montana State Library
Reference Department
1515 E. Sixth Avenue
Helena 59620
406-444-3004

NEBRASKA

University of Nebraska, Lincoln
106 Love Library
Lincoln 68588-0410
402-472-2526

W. Dale Clark Library
Social Sciences Department
215 S. Fifteenth Street
Omaha 68102
402-444-4826

NEVADA

Las Vegas–Clark County Library
   District
1401 E. Flamingo Road
Las Vegas 89109
702-733-7810

Washoe County Library
301 S. Center Street
Reno 89505
702-785-4190

NEW HAMPSHIRE

The New Hampshire Charitable
   Fund
One South Street
Concord 03301
603-225-6641

Littleton Public Library
109 Main Street

Littleton 03561
603-444-5741

NEW JERSEY

Cumberland County Library
800 E. Commerce Street
Bridgeton 08302
609-455-0080

The Support Center
17 Academy Street, Suite 1101
Newark 07102
201-643-5774

County College of Morris
Masten Learning Resource Center
Route 10 and Center Grove Road
Randolph 07869
201-361-5000, ext. 470

New Jersey State Library
Governmental Reference
185 W. State Street
Trenton 08625
609-292-6220

NEW MEXICO

Albuquerque Community Foundation
6400 Uptown Boulevard, N.E., Suite
   500-W
Albuquerque 87110
505-883-6240

New Mexico State Library
300 Don Gaspar Street
Santa Fe 87503
505-827-3824

NEW YORK

New York State Library
Cultural Education Center
Humanities Section
Empire State Plaza

Albany 12230
518-474-7645

Bronx Reference Center
New York Public Library
2556 Bainbridge Avenue
Bronx 10458
212-220-6575

Brooklyn in Touch
101 Willoughby Street, Rm. 1508
Brooklyn 11201
718-237-9300

Buffalo and Erie County Public Library
Lafayette Square
Buffalo 14203
716-856-7525

Huntington Public Library
338 Main Street
Huntington 11743
516-427-5165

Levittown Public Library
Reference Department
One Bluegrass Lane
Levittown 11756
516-731-5728

SUNY/College at Old Westbury Library
223 Store Hill Road
Old Westbury 11568
516-876-3201

Plattsburgh Public Library
Reference Department
15 Oak Street
Plattsburgh 12901
518-563-0921

Adriance Memorial Library
93 Market Street

Poughkeepsie 12601
914-485-4790

Queens Borough Public Library
89-11 Merrick Boulevard
Jamaica 11432
718-990-0700

Rochester Public Library
Business and Social Sciences Division
115 South Avenue
Rochester 14604
716-428-7328

Staten Island Council on the Arts
One Edgewater Plaza, Rm. 311
Staten Island 10305
718-447-4485

Onondaga County Public Library
335 Montgomery Street
Syracuse 13202
315-473-4491

White Plains Public Library
100 Martine Avenue
White Plains 10601
914-682-4488

Suffolk Cooperative Library System
627 N. Sunrise Service Road
Bellport 11713
516-286-1600

NORTH CAROLINA

The Duke Endowment
200 S. Tryon Street, Suite 1100
Charlotte 28202
704-376-0291

Durham County Library
300 N. Roxboro Street

Durham 27701
919-683-2626

North Carolina State Library
109 E. Jones Street
Raleigh 27611
919-733-3270

The Winston Salem Foundation
229 First Union National Bank
   Building
Winston-Salem 27101
919-725-2382

NORTH DAKOTA

Western Dakota Grants Resource
   Center
Bismarck Junior College Library
Bismarck 58501
701-224-5450

The Library
North Dakota State University
Fargo 58105
701-237-8876

OHIO

Public Library of Cincinnati and
   Hamilton County
Education Department
800 Vine Street
Cincinnati 45202
513-369-6940

The Public Library of Columbus
   and Franklin County
Main Library
96 S. Grant Avenue
Columbus, OH 43215
614-222-7151

Dayton and Montgomery County
   Public Library
Social Sciences Division

215 E. Third Street
Dayton 45402-2103
513-224-1651

Toledo–Lucas County Public Library
Social Science Department
325 Michigan Street
Toledo 43624
419-255-7055, ext. 221

Ohio University–Zanesville
Community Education and Development
1425 Newark Road
Zanesville 43701
614-453-0762

Stark County District Library
715 Market Avenue N.
Canton 44702-1080
216-452-0665

OKLAHOMA

Oklahoma City University Library
N.W. Twenty-third at N. Black-
   welder
Oklahoma City 73106
405-521-5072

Tulsa City–County Library System
400 Civic Center
Tulsa 74103
918-592-7944

OREGON

Library Association of Portland
Government and Documents Room
801 S.W. Tenth Avenue
Portland 97205
503-223-7201

Oregon State Library
State Library Building

Salem 97310
503-378-4243

PENNSYLVANIA

Northampton County Area Community College
Learning Resources Center
3835 Green Pond Road
Bethlehem 18017
215-865-5358

Erie County Public Library
3 S. Perry Square
Erie 16501
814-452-2333, ext. 54

Dauphin County Library System
Central Library
101 Walnut Street
Harrisburg 17101
717-234-4961

Lancaster County Public Library
125 N. Duke Street
Lancaster 17602
717-394-2651

The Free Library of Philadelphia
Logan Square
Philadelphia 19103
215-686-5423

Hillman Library
University of Pittsburgh
Pittsburgh 15260
412-624-4423

Economic Development Council of Northeastern Pennsylvania
1151 Oak Street
Pittston 18640
717-655-5581

James V. Brown Library
12 E. Fifty-fourth Street

Williamsport 17701
717-326-0536

RHODE ISLAND

Providence Public Library
Reference Department
150 Empire Street
Providence 02903
401-521-7722

SOUTH CAROLINA

Charleston County Public Library
404 King Street
Charleston 29403
803-723-1645

South Carolina State Library
Reader Services Department
1500 Senate Street
Columbia 29201
803-734-8666

SOUTH DAKOTA

South Dakota State Library
State Library Building
800 N. Illinois Street
Pierre 57501
605-773-3131

Sioux Falls Area Foundation
404 Boyce Greeley Building
321 South Phillips Avenue
Sioux Falls 57102-0781
605-336-7055

TENNESSEE

Knoxville–Knox County Public Library
500 W. Church Avenue
Knoxville 37902
615-523-0781

Memphis–Shelby County Public Library

1850 Peabody Avenue
Memphis 38104
901-725-8876

Public Library of Nashville and
  Davidson County
Eighth Avenue, North and Union
  Street
Nashville 37203
615-244-4700

TEXAS

Amarillo Area Foundation
1000 Polk
P.O. Box 25569
Amarillo 79105-269
806-376-4521

The Hogg Foundation for Mental
  Health
The University of Texas
Austin 78712
512-471-5041

Corpus Christi State University
  Library
6300 Ocean Drive
Corpus Christi 78412
512-991-6810

El Paso Community Foundation
El Paso National Bank Building,
  Suite 1616
El Paso 79901
915-533-4020

Funding Information Center
Texas Christian University Library
Ft. Worth 76129
817-921-7664

Houston Public Library
Bibliographic & Information Center
500 McKinney Avenue

Houston 77002
713-224-5441, ext. 265

Funding Information Library
507 Brooklyn
San Antonio 78215
512-227-4333

Dallas Public Library
Grants Information Service
1515 Young Street
Dallas 75201
214-749-4100

Pam American University
Learning Resource Center
1201 W. University Drive
Edinburg 78539
512-381-3304

UTAH

Salt Lake City Public Library
Business and Science Department
209 E. Fifth Street South
Salt Lake City 84111
801-363-5733

VERMONT

State of Vermont Department of
  Libraries
Reference Services Unit
111 State Street
Montpelier 05602
802-828-3261

VIRGINIA

Grants Resources Library
Hampton City Hall
22 Lincoln Street, Ninth Floor
Hampton 23669
804-727-6496

Richmond Public Library
Business, Science, and Technology
  Department

101 E. Franklin Street
Richmond 23219
804-780-8223

WASHINGTON

Seattle Public Library
1000 Fourth Avenue
Seattle 98104
206-625-4881

Spokane Public Library
Funding Information Center
W. 906 Main Avenue
Spokane 99201
509-838-3361

WEST VIRGINIA

Kanawha County Public Library
123 Capitol Street
Charleston 25301
304-343-4646

WISCONSIN

Marquette University Memorial Library
1415 W. Wisconsin Avenue
Milwaukee 53233
414-224-1515

University of Wisconsin-Madison
  Memorial Library
728 State Street
Madison 53706
608-262-3647

WYOMING

Laramie County Community College Library

1400 E. College Drive
Cheyenne 82007
307-634-5853

CANADA

Canadian Center for Philanthropy
3080 Yonge Street, Suite 4080
Toronto, Ontario M4N3N1
416-484-4118

ENGLAND

Charities Aid Foundation
14 Bloomsbury Square
London WC1A2LP
01-430-1798

MEXICO

Biblioteca Benjamin Franklin
Londres 16
Mexico City 6, D.F.
525-591-0244

PUERTO RICO

Universidad Del Sagrado Corazon
M. M. T. Guevarra Library
Correo Calle Loiza
Santurce 00914
809-728-1515, ext. 274

VIRGIN ISLANDS

College of the Virgin Islands
  Library
Saint Thomas
U.S. Virgin Islands 00801
809-774-9200, ext. 487

The Foundation Center also publishes the *Foundation Directory* listing over 5,000 foundations that have 97% of all foundation assets. *Source Book Profiles*, another center directory, has information about each of the one thousand largest foundations, and the *National Data Book* covers over twenty-two thousand foundations very briefly. There is also a directory of foundations that makes grants to individuals. The Foundation Center provides computer printouts of foundation grants to organizations involved in specific subject areas. These printouts are known as *Comsearch* printouts. There are over one hundred subject categories available. The Foundation Center also offers an index of foundations' previous grants as well as annual reports of foundations. Finally, the center offers an Associates program, where its own researchers are available through WATS lines to do foundation research for an annual fee. Costs of the various sources of information are as follows:

Title	Price
Source Book Profiles, 1987	$850.00
The Foundation Directory, 11th Edition	$ 85.00
The Foundation Grants Index, Annual 15th Edition	$ 44.00
Foundation Grants to Individuals, 5th Edition	$ 18.00
Comsearch Printouts, Paper Edition	$ 17.50 each
Comsearch Printouts, Microfiche Edition	$ 6.00 each
Associates Program	$325.00

DIVERSITY OF FOUNDATIONS

Foundations differ as to their areas of interest and types of grants. Some will fund only "bricks and mortar," or building programs. Some prefer to match money raised from other sources. Some may limit their giving to a specific state or region. Many Texas foundations, for example, give only in Texas. Foundations also differ as to the types of proposals they prefer and as to the number of times during the year when their trustees meet to consider funding requests. There are differences in the political orientation of foundations too, with some liberal and others conservative. Generally, foundations may be categorized as to four types: (1) private foundations, (2) community foundations, (3) corporate foundations, and (4) private operating foundations.

Private foundations may be further categorized according to the size of their assets. The large independent foundations have assets of $100 million or more. The small independent foundations are often family foundations with assets of less than $10 million. These smaller foundations rarely have professional administrative staffs, and they are usually run by family members or attorneys. Large independent foundations generally have large, bureaucratic professional staffs. These foundations often attempt to address broad social problems. Ford Foundation is the largest of these, both in terms of its assets and in total giving.

Waldemar Nielsen's books, *The Big Foundations* in 1972 and *The Golden Donors* in 1985, are like report cards on the work of the largest foundations. Indeed, the earlier book actually caused some foundations to change their personnel and/or their policies. The books provide entertaining glimpses of the personal histories of the founders of each large foundation. They also describe the individuals now responsible for each foundation.

People give to people in foundations, and that simply means that there are unique personalities behind each foundation's funding decisions. The Nielsen books describe some of the more bizarre events in the personal lives of foundation individuals, such as Williametta Keck's feud with her brother, Howard, after Howard allegedly killed her pet ostrich when it got its head caught in a fence hole and he put an orange in the ostrich's mouth, causing it to strangle to death. Any analysis of foundation personalities will inevitably be influenced by regional biases. The Nielsen evaluation found that the worst foundations are located in the Southwest. Also, the second Nielsen book dispels the myths about Texas wealth, pointing out that there is more money in the Northeast. It would be understandable for foundations in the Southwest and Texas to react defensively to the Nielsen analyses.

The demographics of large foundations changed in the years between the two Nielsen books. The greatest growth in the number of large foundations was in California. Community foundations, such as the Cleveland Fund, are now also included among the nation's largest foundations. The Cleveland Fund, in fact, has been the model for new community foundations, which serve the specific area or city where they are located. Community foundations receive the most advantageous tax benefits. A 1985 Council on Foundations survey documented the impressive growth of community foundations: there are more than three hundred with combined assets of $4 billion, (The Nonprofit Times, 1987:13) and the annual grants of community foundations increased from $57 million in 1975 to almost $200 million in 1985 (Council on Foundations 1986c:18). The San Francisco Foundation is the largest community foundation. Community foundation funds may also include corporate contributions, thus making them a viable liaison between different types of grantmakers.

Corporate foundations are the third category of foundations. Unlike corporate contributions programs, these foundations are legal entities separate from the profit-making parent company. However, they may be governed by the parent company's directors or officers. Alcoa is the largest corporate foundation.

The fourth major category of foundations is private operating foundations. These are a hybrid between foundations that give away money and charities that receive money because their funds go only to their own specified organizations. They must meet an IRS income test requiring annual expenditures of the lesser of their adjusted net income or "minimum investment return" directly for the conduct of their tax-exempt purposes. The Robert A. Welch Foundation in Houston is an example of an operating foundation.

COUNCIL ON FOUNDATIONS

All types of foundations are represented in the Council on Foundations in Washington, D.C. The council was founded in 1949. In 1985 its membership included large and small independent foundations (58%), community foundations (18%), corporate foundations and corporate grantmaking programs (16%), operating foundations (4%), public foundations (3%), and international foundations (1%). The council has a thirty-three member Board of Directors, eleven each on three staggered terms. For 1987 the chair of the board was Dwight L. Allison, president of the Boston Foundation, Inc. The other members included sixteen women. There were seven black members and three with Spanish surnames. James A. Joseph, president and chief executive officer of the council, is also black.

The council has a large staff in Washington, D.C. According to its 1986 annual report, the staff included six in international and public affairs, four in government relations and law, four responsible for the council publication *Foundation News*, eleven in administrative and financial services, two in research and planning, and over a dozen working in member services. In addition there were several consultants and specially funded project staff.

The Council on Foundations has five goals:

1. Secure and maintain supportive public policy for philanthropy
2. Promote responsible and effective philanthropy
3. Enhance the understanding of philanthropy in the wider society
4. Support and enhance cooperation among grantmakers
5. Increase the growth of organized philanthropy

In June 1980 the council Board of Directors adopted a statement of principles and practices. Since 1983 all members have been required to endorse the eleven principles and practices:

1. Whatever the nature of the entity engaged in private grantmaking, and whatever its interests, it should seek to establish a set of basic policies that define the program interests and the fundamental objectives to be served.
2. An identifiable board committee, or other decision making body, should have clear responsibility for determining those policies and procedures, causing them to be implemented, and reviewing and revising them from time to time.
3. The processes for receiving, examining, and deciding on grant applications should be established on a clear and logical basis and should be followed in a manner consistent with the organization's policies and purposes.
4. Responsive grantmakers recognize that accountability extends beyond the narrow requirements of the law. Grantmakers should establish and carry out policies that recognize these multiple obligations for accountability: to the charter provisions by which their founders defined certain basic expectations, to those charitable institutions they serve, to the general public, to the Internal Revenue Service, and to certain state governmental agencies.
5. Open communications with the public and with grantseekers about the policies and procedures that are followed in grantmaking is in the interest of all concerned and is important if the grantmaking pro-

cess is to function well, and if trust in the responsibility and account-ability of grantmakers is to be maintained. A brief written statement about politics, program interests, and grantmaking practices, geo-graphic and policy restrictions, and preferred ways of receiving ap-plications is recommended. Prompt acknowledgement of the receipt of any serious application is important. Grantseekers whose pro-grams and proposals [are] outside the interests of the grantmakers should be told immediately and those whose proposals are still under consideration should be informed, insofar as is possible, of the steps and timing that will be taken in reaching the final decision.

6. Beyond the filing of forms required by government, grantmakers should consider possible ways of informing the public concerning their stew-ardship through publication and distribution of periodic reports, preferably annual reports, possibly supplemented by newsletters, re-ports to the Foundation Center, and the use of other communications channels.

7. The preservation and enhancement of an essential community of in-terest between the grantor and the grantee requires that their rela-tionship be based on mutual respect, candor, and understanding with each investing the necessary time and attention to define clearly the purposes of the grant, the expectations as to reports related to finan-cial and other matters, and the provisions for evaluating and publi-cizing projects.

Many grantmakers, going beyond the providing of money, help grantees through such other means as assisting in the sharpening of the objectives, monitoring the performance, evaluating the outcome, and encouraging early planning for future stages.

8. It is important that grantmakers be alert and responsive to changing conditions in society and to the changing needs and merits of partic-ular grantseeking organizations. Responses to needs and social con-ditions may well be determined by independent inquiries, not merely be reactions to requests submitted by grantseekers. In responding to new challenges, grantmakers are helped if they use the special knowl-edge, experience and insight of individuals beyond those persons, families or corporations from which the funds originally came. Some grantmakers find it useful to secure ideas and comments from a va-riety of consultants and advisory panels, as well as diversified staff and board members. In view of the historic underrepresentation of minorities and women in supervisory and policy positions, particular attention should be given to finding ways to draw them into the de-cision-making processes.

9. From time to time, all grantmaking organizations should review their program interests, basic policies, and board and staff composition, and assess the overall results of their grantmaking.

10. Beyond the legal requirements that forbid staff, board members and their families from profiting financially from any philanthropic grant, it is important that grantmakers weigh carefully all circumstances in which there exists the possibility of accusations of self-interest. In particular, staff and board members should disclose to the governing body the nature of their personal or family affiliation or involvement with any organizations for which a grant is considered, even though such affiliation may not give rise to any pecuniary conflict of interest.

11. Grantmakers should maintain interaction with others in the field of philanthropy including such bodies as regional associations of grantmakers, the Foundation Center, the Council on Foundations and various local, regional, and national independent sector organizations. They should bear in mind that they share with others responsibility for strengthening the effectiveness of the many private initiatives to serve the needs and interests of the public and for enhancing general understanding and support of such private initiatives within the community and the nation (Council on Foundations 1984:3).

In order to become a member of the council, foundations and corporations must submit several documents, including a copy of the latest Form 990–PF or Form 990 and a copy of the latest annual report or a letter stating the goals of the grantmaking program. Community foundations must also submit a letter indicating their continuing intention to build and maintain a strong endowment. Public foundations must show that they plan to continue to make at least $100,000 in grants per year and that at least 60% of the budget is devoted to grants, related program costs, and administrative costs for administering grants, that 30% of the budget is for direct grants to multiple individuals or organizations, and that funding is predominantly private rather than public. The annual membership fee for full voting members is $100 per one million in assets to the nearest million, or $100 per $100,000 in grants to the nearest $100,000 if grants exceed 10% of assets. The minimum membership fee is $300. In 1987 the maximum fee for independent and community foundations was $25,000. The maximum fee for corporations, corporate foundations, operating foundations, and public foundations was $7,500. The associate/nonvoting foreign foundation membership fee is $100 for corporations and corporate foundations with charitable distributions less than $1 million and for independent foundations, community foundations, and operating foundations with assets having a market value less than $10 million. The fee is $500 for independent foundations, community foundations, and operating foundations with assets having a market value of $10 million or more and for corporate programs that distribute $1 million or more. First-time members may pay their dues using a graduated formula of 25% the first year, 50% the second year, 75% the third year and full dues the fourth year. In 1986 the number of members in the council was greater than 1,000: 581 independent, 186 community, 42 operating, and 19 foreign foundations, as well as 168 corporate grantmakers and 35 public foundations.

The council offers programs and services in government relations, professional development, technical assistance, communications and public affairs, and research and information. In 1986 the council's total expenses were approximately $4.5 million. Approximately $777,000 was spent for member services, $109,000 for workshops and seminars, $510,000 for the annual conference, $225,000 for research and information services, $662,000 for communications and public affairs, $653,000 for *Foundation News*, $196,000 for legislative activities, and $901,000 for administration and management. Approximately $540,000 was spent for specially funded projects.

In 1985 the council appointed a Long-Range Planning Task Force to project council activities for the next decade. Following meetings with the various council constituencies, the Task Force provided a management-by-objectives type plan for the council, including a mission statement and a statement of objectives and program and management plans. The following statement was reported in the bi-weekly council newsletter of July 22, 1986:

The mission of the Council on Foundations is to promote, encourage and enhance the contributions and responsiveness of organized grantmaking to society and the public good. It functions within organized philanthropy as the national association of grantmaking organizations, serving trustees and staff from independent, corporate, community and public foundations, corporate giving programs and operating foundations. In fulfilling this role, the Council is the principal force in ensuring that those involved in organized grantmaking are provided:

- Representation before and communication with policymakers in government, the media and the general public
- Programs to create new grantmaking organizations and to promote expansion and growth among others
- Education, training, professional development, publications, and related resources
- Research about grantmaking and key issues facing organized philanthropy (Council on Foundations 1986b:3)

The council is extremely active in government relations, representing the concerns of foundations to government officials in Congress, federal agencies, state governments, and the White House. *Washington Update* is the council's periodic newsletter to report on legislative and regulatory issues. For example, the council was active regarding the 1986 tax reform bill, attempting unsuccessfully to preserve the charitable deduction for nonitemizers, endorsing independent sector efforts, and arguing that philanthropy is a public, not a private, benefit.

Also, council attorneys have met with staff of the Joint Committee on Taxation, and they have met with the Assistant Secretary for Tax Policy and with other Treasury Department officials. They have interacted with Treasury officials regarding regulations in several areas: the reduction of the excise tax, the 65% grant administrative cost limit, the 15% administrative cost limit for conduit foundations, the definition of qualified appreciated stock, and the reliance on IRS determination and adjustment of expenditure requirements. The Foundation Lawyers Group, an informal group of attorneys who represent foundations, assisted the council lawyers. John A. Edie, the council general counsel, is a member of the 990 Advisory Committee that advises the IRS regarding Form 990 and Form 990–PF tax returns. He has conducted workshops across the country explaining tax laws to foundation grantmakers, attorneys, and accountants.

For professional development the council offers an annual conference and workshops and seminars for grantmakers. Topics have included leadership, the interrelationship of paid staff and volunteers, and professionalism. The council provides technical assistance to foundations, such as advice on how to start a foundation and on liability insurance for foundation directors. The Charles Stewart Mott Foundation has sponsored the Community Foundation Technical Assistance Program since 1982, and the council has a Committee on Community Foundations. These encourage the growth and development of community foundations. In addition, the council issues a bi-monthly newsletter, *Community Byline*, and it offers a regularly updated *Community Foundation Resource Manual*, with technical assistance and information about items such as investment policies, donor-advised funds, and pooled income funds. Other council publications include *Communications Update*, *International Dateline*, *Regional Review*, and *Washington Update*.

The council has assisted corporate grantmakers with workshops on such topics as the tension between the views of corporate philanthropy as a marketing tool or as part of a moral obligation. The council's technical assistance includes providing information regarding alternate investment strategies, such as program related investments (PRI). Examples of PRI include community development credit unions, minority banks, low income housing finance, enterprise incubators, and cooperatives.

In 1986 there were nineteen international foundations on the council's membership roster: Aleman (Miguel) Foundation, Buckland (William) Foundation, Calgary Foundation, Donner Canadian Foundation, Graele Foundation, Hong Kong Pei Hau Education Foundation, Inlaks Foundation, Ivey (Richard) Foundation, Law Foundation of British Columbia, Luso American Development Foundation, McConnell (J. W.) Foundation, Inc., Metropolitan Toronto Community Foundation, Muttart (Gladys and Merrill) Foundation, Resource Group, Spiro (Fundacao Carl E. Durga), Toyota Foundation, Utah Foundation, Victoria Community Foundation, and Winnipeg Foundation. The council also has an international program which includes serving as an information clearinghouse for grantmakers about events such as the Ethiopian famine and Mexico City earthquake and assisting in international conferences. For example, the council and SOLIDARIOS (Council of Latin American Foundations) cosponsored a conference on "The Role of the Private Sector in Promoting Social and Economic Progress in Latin America and the Caribbean." Council members have also met with members of the European Hague Club, with the Netherlands Bernard Van Leer Foundation executives making a presentation in those meetings. Council representatives have hosted Japanese foundation officials. They also helped to plan and participated in the Aga Khan Conference on "Effective Private Sector Contribution to Development in Sub Saharan Africa" held in Nairobi, Kenya. The chair of the International Grantmaking Committee, Richard Lyman, president of the Rockefeller Foundation, led council attendees. The council's publication, *Foundation News*, has included a European correspondent based in Paris. Among his articles was a cover story on the growth of organized philanthropy in Europe. The quarterly council newsletter, *International Dateline*, provides information to members about international opportunities.

The council has also interacted with religious grantmakers. It conducted a survey and issued a report on "The Philanthropy of Organized Religion," and it has sponsored dialogues between foundation and religious representatives on issues such as funding religious organizations, and the black church and philanthropy. It also assists endowed churches in their grantmaking.

Foundation News is the primary council publication. In 1986 the magazine acquired *Grantsmanship Center News*, increasing its circulation from over 15,000 to 22,500. The *Foundation News* appeals to readers on both sides of the desk in philanthropy, from fund raisers for nonprofit organizations to foundation trustees. The *Foundation News* staff produced the council's 1985 Annual Report, which won first prize in design and content from the Society of National Association Publications. The council actively pursues media relations, helping to educate reporters about philanthropy. The council collaborates with the Communications Network in Philanthropy to help improve communications, such as annual reports by grantmakers.

The council's research has also included collaboration with the Yale Program on Non-Profit Organizations in their study on the formation, growth, and termination of foundations—the "births and deaths" study. In addition, the council interfaces with the research efforts of organizations such as the National Center for Charitable Statistics, the Independent Sector, and the American

Association of Fund-Raising Counsel. Council researchers assist foundations in personnel issues too, including an annual survey of personnel and salaries. The council has also cooperated with other special interest or affinity groups, such as Hispanics in Philanthropy, the National Network of Grantmakers, Grantmakers in Health, and the Association of Black Foundation Executives. Finally, the council has surveyed regional associations of grantmakers to compare their policies and procedures. The following is a list of such regional associations:

CALIFORNIA

Northern California Grantmakers—*San Francisco, California*

San Diego Grantmakers Group

Southern California Association for Philanthropy—*Los Angeles, California*

COLORADO

Association of Colorado Foundations—*Denver, Colorado*

CONNECTICUT

Coordinating Council for Foundations—*Hartford, Connecticut*

GEORGIA

Southeastern Council of Foundations—(Alabama, Arkansas, Florida, Georgia, Kentucky, Louisiana, Mississippi, North Carolina, South Carolina, Tennessee, and Virginia)—*Atlanta, Georgia*

ILLINOIS

Donors Forum of *Chicago*

INDIANA

Indiana Donors Alliance c/o Indiana Committee for the Humanities—*Indianapolis, Indiana*

MARYLAND

Association of *Baltimore* Area Grantmakers

MASSACHUSETTS

Associated Grantmakers of Massachusetts—*Boston, Massachusetts*

MICHIGAN

Council of Michigan Foundations—*Grand Haven, Michigan*

MINNESOTA

Minnesota Council on Foundations—*Minneapolis, Minnesota*

MISSOURI

Clearinghouse for Midcontinent Foundations—*Kansas City, Missouri*

Metropolitan Association for Philanthropy—*St. Louis, Missouri*

NEW JERSEY

Council of New Jersey Grantmakers—*East Orange, New Jersey*

NEW YORK

New York Regional Association of Grantmakers—*New York, New York*

Rochester Grantmakers Forum

Grantmakers of Western New York—*Buffalo, New York*

OHIO

Donors Forum of Ohio—*Dayton, Ohio*

PENNSYLVANIA

Grantmakers of Western Pennsylvania—*Pittsburgh, Pennsylvania*

TEXAS

Conference of Southwest Foundations—(Arizona, Arkansas, Nevada, New
    Mexico, Oklahoma, and Texas)—*Corpus Christi, Texas*

WASHINGTON

Pacific Northwest Grantmakers Forum—*Seattle, Washington*

WISCONSIN

Foundation Forum of Wisconsin—*Milwaukee, Wisconsin*

LEGAL ISSUES

Foundations are required to give away a certain percentage of
their assets each year as contributions. The 1969 Patman congressional hearings scrutinized foundations giving to make certain,
among other things, that foundation directors were not lining their
own pockets with money. Many foundations make contributions
only to tax-exempt organizations, and therefore, fund raisers need
to be certain their organization has been given IRS 501(c)(3) status. (An exception is the MacArthur Foundation that sponsored

Waldemar Nielsen's second book. It gives annual contributions to individuals through its much-publicized MacArthur Fellows program in which individual "geniuses" are nominated by an elite committee to receive income to help support them in various creative endeavors. The second Nielsen book also mentions a unique case in 1974, when the Hearst Foundation got a special IRS ruling to allow it to pay a $1.5 million ransom for Patty Hearst, the kidnapped daughter of one of the trustees, to the Symbionese Liberation Army because the kidnappers claimed the charitable purpose of feeding the poor.

Foundations are prohibited from lobbying. Yet certainly foundations are involved in public policy issues. The second Nielsen book includes an analysis of the public policy grants of several of the largest foundations. The Council on Foundations has prepared a guidance memorandum of pitfalls for foundations to avoid, along with twenty-five case histories. At its 1985 Annual Conference, the council hosted a dinner discussion by Representative Charles B. Rangel (D-NY), Chairman of the House Ways and Means Subcommittee on Oversight, and Senator David Durenberger (R-MN) on the role of foundations in the formulation of public policy. James Joseph, president of the council, wrote in the 1985 Annual Report:

> The 1,500 grantmakers who participated in the Council's 1985 Annual Conference heard members of the tax-writing committees of the U.S. Congress and Representatives of the Reagan Administration urge them to contribute more actively to the public policymaking process.
>
> This intertwining of philanthropy with public policy is far from universally accepted, but the national concern with tax policy makes this an especially good time for the grantmaking community to carefully examine what connection is appropriate.
>
> The use of philanthropy to intervene in the life of the community is a practice that extends as far back as early Egyptian, Roman and Greek societies. While a private foundation is strictly forbidden by federal law from making expenditures to influence an election, it is encouraged to affect more general public policy in certain prescribed ways:
>
> 1. By engaging in or funding nonpartisan analysis, study or research and by making the results available to the public or to legislators.
> 2. By responding to written requests for technical advice or assistance from legislative committees; or

3. By expending funds or making grants for the examination and discussion of broad social, economic and similar problems as long as such discussion does not address the merits of specific legislative proposals.

Tradition alone is not a warrant for foundations to operate in the public policy arena, but it is important to remember that the practice is neither new nor simply the result of encouragement by the present leadership in the Congress or at the White House.

Early this century, Rockefeller philanthropies attacked major public health problems that then lay outside the domain of public policy. During the interwar period, several major foundations sought actively to stimulate actions by local governments—the Duke Endowment in hospital development and the care of orphans; the Commonwealth Fund in child guidance, health and housing; and W. K. Kellogg in the reform of child welfare practices.

On the eve of World War II the Carnegie Corporation gave birth to a scrupulously documented, deeply analytical study—Gunnar Myrdal's *An American Dilemma*—that focused a new spotlight on the massive failure of public policy in the field of racial justice. The effects of the engagement of grantmaking and operating foundations with public policy continue to be seen widely and deeply—in legislation, in court decisions, in public attitudes and in social changes across a wide front.

Private foundations today are grappling with some of the most vexing public issues of the day—from budget deficits to tax simplification and reform, from nuclear proliferation to agricultural and industrial dislocation, from welfare policy to regulatory reform.

The present issue, then, is not whether foundations should contribute to public policy, but how to do so in ways that are helpful to the public and do not confuse charitable intent with partisan political purpose. Some foundations will continue to avoid any involvement with government and those who make public policy. This conscious choice reflects the pluralism of the grantmaking sector. But for those who choose to make a contribution in this area it may be useful to consider a few guidelines that grow out of the experience of foundations already active in the public policy arena:

Work from a solid base of facts and analysis. The currency in which society expects foundations to deal is information and insight, not propaganda, not unsupported opinion, not militant partisanship.

Deal with issues with which you have experience. Policymakers are more likely to pay attention to an organization familiar with the realities and complexities of a particular field.

Recognize that public policy involves the political process. No matter how certain a foundation is of its disinterested, objective stance, to enter the policy process is to enter the political arena, in which not all players necessarily regard other players as spokespersons for the public interest.

Be prepared to stay the course. If a policy issue is important enough to address, it is worth working for over a sustained period. Quick fixes and hasty retreats are inimical to the foundation habit of foresight and persistence.

Keep an open mind and a readiness to compromise. Perfect solutions are uncommon in the messy interplay of forces in public policy formulation.

Work with others. It pays to have company in public policy efforts, not simply for the comfort of numbers but principally for the additional experience, wisdom and credibility others have to offer.

Accept the consequences. The principle of accountability counts for very little if it does not embrace every action a foundation takes, every organization it supports.

Obey the law. Direct expenditures to lobby or influence legislation are strictly prohibited; however, foundations may lobby in their own defense without penalty on matters that affect their own existence. Foundations may also affect general public policy in many ways specifically authorized by law.

In the present stage of interaction among grantmakers, the foundation that wants to take the first step into the terrain of public policy can turn to others who have worked the territory for many years. The Council on Foundations is also well prepared to help, through its professional resources and by virtue of its own rich experience in the corridors where public policies are debated and decided (Council on Foundations 1986c:3).

As a result of the Patman hearings in 1969, many foundations were required to divest themselves of very large holdings of shares of stock in their associated companies by 1989. In 1983 more than twelve foundations sought special exemptions from the divestiture requirements. The resulting 1983 congressional hearings differed from those in 1969 because there was a more positive attitude among Congressmen toward foundations. Yet public suspicion of foundations still exists. For example, the *Houston Post* covered a state attorney general's investigation of Texas' largest foundations with stories such as this:

The giant philanthropic foundations whose namesakes dominate the Houston landscape—Brown, Cullen, Wortham, M. D. Anderson, Hermann, Moody, Jesse Jones—do much more than simply determine which museum or university gets what grant: they perpetuate the power and influence of Houston's long-dead founding fathers.

An examination of the inner workings of these large charitable trusts has uncovered an interlocking circle of power driven by a select group of law firms and banks, which profit from their connections.

It also revealed a choice group of beneficiaries of the foundations—which were created in the wills and special indentures of the wealthy. Those getting large grants frequently have had connections to the foundations trustees, who often are the descendants, lawyers and business associates of the founders.

All this concentrated power has drawn the attention of Texas Attorney General, Jim Mattox, who has started a long-range investigation looking for possible self-dealing, abuse of power, breach of fiduciary duties, disregard for the original purposes of a foundation and other possible violations of the intent and nature of these charitable foundations (*Houston Post* 1985:1A, copyright 1985, *Houston Post* excerpts reprinted by permission).

EFFECTS OF THE 1986 TAX ACT

The Tax Reform Act of 1986 contains provisions affecting the foundation community. The law does not include a controversial provision for a dividends paid deduction that the Council on Foundations had actively opposed. It would have cost at least a half-dozen council members more than $1 million annually in new taxes. The provision would have required all charitable institutions owning more than 5% of a company to pay unrelated business income tax on 10% of the dividends from that company.

The 1986 tax law corrected an error in the Tax Reform Act of 1984. The 1984 law allowed private foundations to reduce their excise tax on net investment income from 2% to 1% if they met certain conditions. One condition required a foundation to meet in the current year a payout percentage equal to the average payout of the previous five years, but if the average was less than 5%, a foundation was ineligible for the reduction. Congress intended for the requirement to rule out only those foundations who failed to pay out the 5% minimum for any of the previous five years, but for technical reasons a foundation could be below the 5% without violating the requirement. The 1986 law corrected that error. The correction saved more than $1 million in taxes in 1985 for some foundations (Council on Foundations 1987:10).

The 1986 law requires private foundations, beginning in 1987, to pay their taxes quarterly on an estimated basis, thus costing foundations $6 million to $7 million in foregone revenue. In addition, the law imposes restrictions on the pension program most common to foundations. Finally, the 1986 law's treatment of gifts of appreciated property, whereby individuals and corporations subject to the alternative minimum tax are permitted only to deduct cost, may jeopardize the growth of community foundations and may also discourage those desiring to form new foundations during their lifetimes.

PERSONAL EXPERIENCES

When I was a graduate student in social work at the University of Texas in Austin I had my first interaction with a foundation. In one course we reviewed and evaluated grant proposals to the Moody Foundation and made recommendations to the representative of the three-member Moody Board of Directors. The Hogg Foundation for Mental Health (yes, there really was a woman named Ima Hogg) also allowed our class to review their grant requests.

This class exercise demonstrated that both the Moody and the Hogg Foundations were open to public scrutiny. As social work students, we were somewhat liberal in our political outlook. Yet those foundations allowed themselves to be vulnerable to our critiques. I would like to see more foundations offer the opportunity for the kind of exercise we had in that social work class.

That exercise allowed us to step into the shoes of the donor. We could understand better after the exercise the complexities of giving grants. We saw the difficulty, for example, in choosing between several worthwhile projects. We understood the foundations' need to prioritize their gifts and to focus their funding on specific target areas. By stepping into the shoes of the foundation grantmaker we, as future social workers who could easily become executive directors of social work agencies seeking foundation funds, were better prepared not only to empathize with foundation grantmakers but also to successfully communicate funding needs to foundations.

My next interaction with foundations came just after I had completed graduate school. I was selected to participate in two three-week United Nations programs, one in Geneva, Switzerland, and one at the United Nation's headquarters in New York. I typed my budget for travel, room, and board on a single sheet of paper and found an outdated *Foundation Directory* in Houston's old downtown library. I was not professional in my attempt to find a Houston foundation to pay for my participation in the U.N. programs. I even telephoned contact persons before they had seen my budget or requested an interview. Nonetheless, it was near the end of the workday when a Houston lawyer, Alvin Owsley, Jr., agreed to see me and to talk about my funding request from his family foundation, the Owsley Foundation. After we had met and talked he agreed to provide the funds to the University of Texas Graduate School of Social Work to disburse to me. The school in turn requested that I write a report for them about the U.N. programs. I also wrote a report for Mr. Owsley. Ironically, I later read in a book that the founder of the Owsley Foundation, Mr. Owsley's father, had been an outspoken critic and opponent of the United Nations.

My third interaction with foundations occurred when I was helping to raise funds for the After Dinner (A.D.) Players, Jeannette Clift George's Christian Theater Company in Houston. Mrs. George was the actress who played a Dutch woman named Corrie ten Boom in a Billy Graham movie about the Holocaust, *The Hiding Place*. I helped prepare funding proposals for foundations, but the best fund raising for the A.D. Players occurred when Mrs. George met in person with potential donors. The A.D. Players' contributions now include about twenty foundations, and they have employed a full-time development person during the last few years.

My most extensive contact with foundations occurred when I was a contributions analyst for Pennzoil in Houston. We corporate grantmakers and some foundation grantmakers met monthly for lunch at the Houston Club under the auspices of the Houston Group, an organization sponsored by the Better Business Bureau, to review our responses to funding requests. I also interacted with foundation grantmakers at the various luncheons and dinners where

we were all solicited for donations, and at workshops and conferences about philanthropy.

I had the opportunity to visit a foundation, Lilly Endowment in
Indianapolis, when I joined board members of the National Association of Christians in Social Work (NACSW) at a meeting with
Charles Johnson at Lilly Endowment to receive not only money
but also consultation about NACSW's development program. Lilly
Endowment paid for our travel, room, and board. The NACSW
board member who initiated the contact with Lilly Endowment
was an officer with the Salvation Army in Indianapolis.

My most recent interactions with foundations have been through
the "Successful Fund Raising" undergraduate course I teach at Oral
Roberts University. The following is a list of guest speakers from
foundations:

Dr. Tom Broce—President, Kerr Foundation, Norman, Oklahoma

J. A. Diana—Vice President for Administration and Treasurer, John D.
and Catherine T. MacArthur Foundation, Chicago

Dr. Manning M. Pattillo—President, Oglethorpe College, formerly President, The Foundation Center

Donald P. Moyers—Vice Chairman and Trustee Mabee Foundation, Tulsa

Jessye Payne—Consultant, W. Clement and Jessie V. Stone Foundation,
Chicago

Valleau Wilkie, Jr.—Executive Vice President, Sid W. Richardson Foundation, Fort Worth, Texas, and past Chairman of the Council on Foundations

A major assignment I give my students is for them to select a
foundation and to report about it, making a personal visit to the
foundation office if possible or at least telephoning the foundation. The students generally select their foundations from the
Foundation Directory. Most foundations have been cordial and
helpful to the students, but a few have been suspicious that the
students were fund raisers and a very small number have been
rude, refusing to give the students any information. Hopefully, as
more universities offer courses about philanthropy, all foundations will be more accessible to college students and more eager
for the opportunity to help strengthen the students' education about
the work of foundations.

RESUMÉ OF A FOUNDATION EXECUTIVE

RICHARD W. LYMAN, PRESIDENT
THE ROCKEFELLER FOUNDATION

SPECIAL FIELD: Contemporary British History with a specialization in the Labour Party.

EDUCATION:

1947 B.A. Swarthmore College (History, with high honors)
1948 M.A. Harvard University (History)
1954 Ph.D. Harvard University (History)

HONORARY DEGREES AND AWARDS

1971 LL.D. Washington University
1972 LL.D. Mills College
1974 LL.D. Swarthmore College
1975 D.H.L. University of Rochester
1975 LL.D. Yale University
1978 Officer de la Legion d'honneur (France)
1980 LL.D. Harvard University
Fellow Royal Historical Society
Honorary Fellow London School of Economics

EXPERIENCE

1943-46	U.S. Army Air Force
1949-51	Teaching Fellow (History) Harvard University
1951-52	Fulbright Fellow, London School of Economics
1952-53	Instructor (History) Swarthmore College
1953-54	Instructor (History) Washington University, St. Louis
1953-66	Special Correspondent, The Economist, London
1954-58	Assistant Professor (History) Washington University
1958-62	Associate Professor (History) Stanford University
1962-80	Professor (History) Stanford University
1964-67	Associate Dean, School of Humanities and Sciences, Stanford University
1967-70	Vice President and Provost, Stanford University
1970-80	President, Stanford University
1980-	President Emeritus, Stanford University
1980-	J.E. Wallace Sterling Professor of Humanities Emeritus, Stanford University
1980-	President, The Rockefeller Foundation

PROFESSIONAL ACTIVITIES	1947-48	Hannah Leedom Fellowship (given by Swarthmore College for 1st year graduate work)
	1951-52	Fulbright Fellowship in England
	1958-61	Member, Board of Editors, Journal of Modern History, published at University of Chicago
	1958-62	Visiting Honors Examiner, Swarthmore College; Chairman of History Examiners, 1962
	1959-60	Guggenheim Fellowship
	1967-69	Member, Policyholders Nominating Committee, TIAA-CREF
	1971-74	Member, Advisory Committee on Planning and Institutional Programs, National Science Foundation
	1972-80	Member, Executive Committee, Association of American Universities; Chairman, 1978-79
	1974-77	Chairman, Council on Federal Relations, Association of American Universities
	1976-76	Member, American Council of Learned Societies, Associate Visiting Committee
	1976-77	Member of the Board, National Association of Independent Colleges and Universities
	1976-82	Member, National Council for the Humanities; Vice Chairman, 1980-82
	1976-82	Trustee, The Carnegie Foundation for the Advancement of Teaching
	1976-	Trustee, The Rockefeller Foundation
	1976-	Member, National Committee on United States-China Relations
	1978-80	Chairman, Commission on the Humanities
	1978-	Director, International Business Machines Corporation
	1980-	Member of the Board, Independent Sector; Chairperson, 1983-
	1981-	Director, The Chase Manhattan Bank, NA and the Chase Manhattan Corporation
	1982-	Member of the Board, Council on Foundations

ORGANIZATIONS: Phi Beta Kappa
American Association of University Professors
American Historical Association
Conference on British Studies (New York)

Society for the Study of Labour History (London)
Association of Contemporary Historians
Council on Foreign Relations

PUBLICATIONS: The First Labour Government, 1924 (London, 1957; re-issued, New York, 1975)
Major Crises in Western Civilization, (co-editor with Lewis W. Spitz), 2 vols., New York, Harcourt, Brace & World, Inc., 1965
Author of numerous articles and reviews in his field.

PERSONAL DATA: Born: October 19, 1923, Philadelphia, PA

Married: Elizabeth Schauffler Lyman (Known as Jing Lyman), 1947

Children: Jennifer (1950)
Holly Antolini (1952)
Christopher (1955)
Timothy (1957)

5

United Way

INTRODUCTION

The concept of consolidated fund drives in the United States is over one hundred years old. The United Way is the most popular consolidated campaign. Its mission is "to increase the organized capacity of people to care for one another." There is a national United Way office, but each community's local United Way is autonomous. Volunteers guided by professional staff are vital to United Way success. The "people give to people" dimension occurs both in the United Way fund drives and in the allocation of United Way funds. United Way membership is important to many nonprofit organizations. However, nonprofit organizations that are not members of the United Way have formed their own alternative federated campaigns to compete with the United Way at the workplace.

HISTORY AND ORGANIZATION

The United Way concept originated in Denver in 1887 when four clergymen consolidated the fund drives of twenty-two agencies in their community into the Charity Organization Society. Associated Charities was the fund raising branch of the society. It distributed $17,880.03 in 1888, but in 1893 the society was a victim of the silver panic. By 1895 there were more than one hundred charity organization societies in the Unitd States. In 1913 in Cleveland the Federation of Charity and Philanthropy was another United Way–type effort. The United Way concept evolved through Community Chests, United Funds, United Community Services, and Torch Drives in the 1920s, 1930s, and 1940s. Organized labor has supported such efforts since 1942 when officers of the AFL and CIO signed an agreement with Community Chests and Councils officers. Business and labor leaders view the United Way as a means to maximize the efficiency of charitable fund raising.

In 1976, United Way of America's Program for the Future set a goal of increasing support by 11% annually over ten years. After setting the goal, the actual increase was 8% in 1976, 9.1% in 1977, 9.4% in 1978, and 8% in 1979. The 1978 increase was the greatest in twenty-two years. In 1986 the United Way raised about $2.44 billion for health and social services, up from over $1.5 billion in 1980. In April 1987 the United Way launched its "Second Century Initiative," an effort to double its funding and volunteers by 1991. The plan calls for United Way to double the 334 companies it works with. Corporate acquisitions and mergers have caused a decrease in the number of corporations. United Way traditionally worked with companies having an average of forty thousand employees, but now it seeks to include more companies with five thousand employees and even some with fifteen hundred employees. United Way also seeks entrepreneurial companies and regional utilities as well as high-income individuals such as doctors and lawyers, and United Way seeks more in-kind gifts such as food, clothing, computers, and transportation.

The national United Way office is located at 701 North Fairfax Street, Alexandria, VA 22314-2045, 703-836-7100. There are over two thousand United Way offices across the United States and nearly two hundred in other countries. In the United States, each is incorporated as a tax-exempt 501(c)(3) organization. Each community's United Way coordinates its own campaign and disburses the funds itself among its own human services agencies.

The national United Way of America is a nonprofit membership association composed of the autonomous local United Ways. It offers services in the areas of volunteer and professional training, fund raising, planning, allocations, government relations, labor relations, communications, national agency relations, research, and data collection. It also provides model programs and guidelines to improve local United Ways. Since 1970 the president of United Way of America and United Way International has been William Aramony, who has a business degree and a master's degree in social work. The membership organization, United Way of America, does not raise or allocate funds, but it receives dues from member United Ways across the country. There is a "fair share" dues formula based on the amount each local United Way raises for itself.

The United Way's administrative costs average less than 10%. This includes administration expenses of such management activities as board and committee meetings; office management; internal accounting, auditing and budgeting; personnel procurement and purchasing supplies; and allocations and agency relations expenses such as review of agency budgets and ongoing daily assistance to member agencies. The cost of fund raising also includes payroll for fund raising staff, fund raising public relations materials, and expenses of training and recruiting volunteers and offering fund raising clinics and workshops.

United Way agencies must report their budgets to the United Way according to a specified format. United Ways use accounting principles of the American Institute of Certified Public Accountants. Also, the United Ways themselves must have annual audits by independent public accountants. They are encouraged to publish financial reports, including campaign results, to the public.

PROFESSIONAL STAFF AND MANAGEMENT TRAINEES

The United Way prides itself in being a volunteer organization. Although there are paid staff members, volunteers help with the fund drives and allocation of funds. The paid staff have backgrounds in such disciplines as social planning, communications, and management. Of course, volunteers also serve on United Ways' boards of directors across the nation.

United Way professionals work in four areas: (1) community problem solving, (2) fund raising, (3) allocations, and (4) communications. Community problem solvers gather data about social problems in communities. They work with neighborhood groups to identify needs, and they work with volunteers to offer alternative solutions. They coordinate services with private and government agencies. The only direct client contact may be by administering an information and referral service or voluntary action center.

United Way fund raisers assist volunteers who encourage others to give time and money to the United Way. They work with business, labor, and community leaders. They may use marketing approaches to appeal to specific audiences.

Allocations professionals assist the volunteers making allocations decisions. They help review agency budgets. They work with agency professionals, helping their operations.

United Way professionals in communications also assist volunteers. They do public relations for the United Way through the media and publications. They also prepare special presentations and speakers' bureaus.

United Way provides regular training for its professionals through its National Academy for Volunteerism. The academy offers courses in the four areas of United Way professional activity and in management. It is possible to have lifetime careers in the over eight hundred United Ways that have full-time staffs. The size of the staff depends on the size of the community. Salaries and benefits vary depending on the United Way location and the size of its budget. Most top executives in large cities have salaries over $100,000. United Way career professionals may be promoted within one United Way or they may be promoted by changing to another United Way in another community. There are about five thousand United Way professionals.

The United Way Management Training Program began in 1974. Its purpose is to provide intensive, accelerated training for individuals preparing for professions in the United Way and to assure the continual availability of such highly qualified professionals. Trainees have an orientation session at the United Way's national headquarters in Alexandria, Virginia. During the orientation, they have an overview of United Way community problem solving, communications, campaigns, and allocations.

Trainees then serve with placements at local United Way organizations, where they are supervised but are treated as regular professional staff members. Trainees receive salaries and fringe benefits commensurate with their experience and educational backgrounds. No annual salary is less than $18,000. The United Way also pays certain travel expenses for the trainees. Moving and storage expenses must be negotiated and approved in advance.

Acceptance of a traineeship obligates the trainee to accept employment with the United Way immediately upon completion of the program. Trainees must be available for relocation. To be eligible to be a trainee the applicant must have a bachelor's degree, high academic standing, leadership ability, effective oral and written communication skills, and career concern and motivation.

FUND RAISING AND ALLOCATION OF FUNDS

At first it might appear that the United Way is an exception to the idea of "people give to people." However, the interpersonal dimension is as much a part of United Way funding as it is of other types of funding. In fact, personal interaction occurs at two levels in United Way funding. One level originates with the United Way staff and volunteers. A typical campaign will have paid staff who organize a hierarchy of volunteers, starting with a campaign chairman who is an influential member of the business community, moving to a central committee whose members each have their own committee, and branching out from there to other committees and finally to individual employees of corporations. At each level interpersonal interaction is important. The United Way staff must be able to motivate and encourage the chairman and his committee not only to contribute money on behalf of themselves and/or their corporations but also to motivate their own committees who in turn motivate others. The United Way staff helps by providing brochures and audiovisual materials, but the solicitation is generally one-on-one.

There is an ethical issue at this level of United Way fund raising. The danger is that the motivation for giving will be solely a high-pressure "arm twisting" at the workplace. Businesses may compete among themselves to raise the greatest contributions and pledges from their employees. The president of the company may put pressure on his vice presidents, who pressure their managers, who in turn pressure their supervisors to strongly encourage employee gifts and pledges. Individual employee responses may not remain confidential. It is possible that a company's commitment to the United Way campaign could even be indicated by the hierarchical status of the person who solicits employee donations. In order to counteract such coercion, the United Way Board of Governors and local United Way boards have adopted formal policy statements against coercion. They encourage peer solicitation instead of manager solicitation. They may also discourage the practice of seeking 100% participation in a campaign. The United Way Board of Governors states: "Giving is a personal matter. Whether individuals wish to give and how much they choose to give are up to the individual. . . . No form of coercion is acceptable, particularly that which includes any stated or implied effect on personal employment status" (United Way 1987:2).

The other level of interpersonal interaction in United Way funding occurs between the social service agencies receiving funding and the United Way staff and volunteers who decide the annual allocation of dollars among the agencies. Each year the various United Way agencies submit their budget requests to their local United Way. The local United Way determines its annual campaign goal by the total amount of funding requested by its member agencies. The competition for funds is keen.

United Way volunteers help decide the allocation of funds raised in the campaign. A United Way brochure includes the following simulation game:

Directions: Each of the ten services below needs $200, but allocate a total of just $1,000 among them:

Character building programs	$_____
Day Care	$_____
Elderly Services	$_____
Emergency Aid for Poor and Needy	$_____
Family and Individual Counseling	$_____
Health Services	$_____
Information and Referral	$_____
Programs to Prevent Abuse	$_____
Recreation Programs	$_____
Work and Training for the Handicapped	$_____
Total	$1,000

Of course, the actual allocations process includes much more information about specific agencies, but the simulation is valuable in demonstrating the difficulty of making allocations decisions. United Ways support over thirty-seven thousand agencies nationwide, with support averaging 20 percent to 25% of the income of member agencies. 1986 allocations nationally were approximately 53% family service, 2.9% special and supplementary education, 5% job training and placement, 8% disaster relief and crime prevention, 6.4% volunteer and social service coordination, 3.6% food and shelter, and 21.1% health.

The interpersonal dimension of receiving United Way monies begins when an agency first applies for United Way membership. Each United Way may differ in its requirements for new members. However, there are basic requirements that usually must be met. Among these is the ability of the representatives of the agency to convince the United Way staff that they will be responsible professionals. How do they come across in the first meeting? Do they appear confident and trustworthy? Are they competent to serve their clients? If the agency representatives have already developed a rapport with the United Way staff they will be better able to convince them that their agency is suitable for United Way membership.

Once initial membership is approved, the social service agencies must submit budget requests each year. In Tulsa, for example, volunteer contributions committees approve all or parts of these budgets. There is a three-year term for volunteers. I served as a volunteer on one of these contributions committees, and I observed there the interpersonal dimensions at this level of solicitation. The first contact between committee members and agency representatives usually occurred when the committee members were given a tour of the agency. First impressions began with impressions of the agency representative who provided the tour. This person's comments and conduct at the agency were very important in determining the committee's response to the agency's budget. The next encounter usually occurred at the United Way headquarters. There a United Way staff person helped to conduct an interview of agency representatives by committee members. The agency representatives were often "on the hot seat" as they answered specific questions about items in their budget. It was essential that the agency representatives be comfortable talking about numbers and capable of translating social service jargon into terms that the volunteers on the committee could understand. Our committee was

comprised mainly of business people, including an attorney and/
or accountant who usually chaired the committee. The committee
would then vote on the budget and present its recommendation to
the United Way staff.

Further interpersonal interaction occurred between the committee and the United Way staff. The United Way executives made
the final decision about the budget recommendations. Therefore,
agency representatives who received negative committee recommendations could still hope for approval of their budgets if their
interpersonal relationships with United Way executives were
stronger than the committee's relationships to the United Way executives.

CHALLENGES TO THE UNITED WAY

United Way funding is necessary for most social service agencies. The United Way endorsement means community acceptance.
Critics have charged, however, that it is too difficult for new or
controversial agencies to receive United Way funding. For example, abortion opponents have been able to end United Way membership of abortion agencies and support groups by threatening to
discontinue all United Way contributions in their communities. The
controversy regarding the United Way funding of abortion services has received much publicity, as has the funding of family
planning programs.

The United Way response to the charge that it is difficult for
new agencies to become members is that United Ways serve new
agencies through management assistance and direct consultation
as well as through financial assistance. Some United Ways set aside
a portion of campaign funds for new programs, and some provide
special grants to help enable newer agencies to get established.
United Ways also help link business volunteers that have accounting, budgeting, planning, research, and other management skills
with new agencies to help those agencies meet the standards for
initial United Way financial support. There is also United Way
assistance to new agencies through recruiting and training volunteers to help with the new agencies' programs and to develop
funding and other resources for them.

Once an agency receives United Way membership and funding,

it must abide by the United Way's funding regulations. It must submit its annual budget by a deadline and in the required form. It must have United Way approval of any additional fund raising activities other than the United Way campaign. It may not be able to accept additional funds from other sources without United Way approval. Yet, United Ways do not want to support more than a portion of an agency's budget, thus necessitating that the agency secure additional funds. It may be discouraging for United Way agencies to solicit additional funding from a corporation only to be told that the corporation's United Way gift, often matching its employees' gifts, was all that the corporation intended to contribute to any United Way agency.

The National Committee for Responsive Philanthropy has participated in many challenges to what it perceives as a United Way monopoly of access to funding. For example, it joined with the Media Access Project to file a fairness doctrine complaint with the Federal Communications Commission arguing that it was unfair for United Ways to have access to $20 million of public service announcement time during National Football League games whereas there was no time provided for agencies that were not members of United Ways. The FCC complaint was filed after an unsuccessful attempt to convince the networks to voluntarily resolve the problem (National Committee for Responsive Philanthropy 1980:1).

Despite United Way acceptance of designated gifts, special interest groups continue to challenge the United Way. The Brown Lung Association fought for United Way acceptance of its member chapters, charging that United Way boards opposed the chapters' membership because textile industry executives served on United Way boards. There has also been criticism of United Way's relationship to minorities. For example, a 1980 National Committee for Responsive Philanthropy newsletter cites a Norfolk State University study that found that although 95% of minority banks supported United Ways, only 27% (sixteen of sixty) of those banks had deposits from United Way and those deposits were relatively small (National Committee for Responsive Philanthropy 1980:6).

The creation of the Black United Fund to compete with the United Way for workplace funding is a result of such criticism. Yet, the United Way argues that it does indeed serve minorities. First it argues that its general support of traditional programs such as Boy

Scouts, the Salvation Army, settlement houses, and Travelers Aid includes work in minority communities. It also argues that its services include medical research about such diseases as sickle-cell anemia. Also the United Way argues that it helps provide technical and management assistance to minority agencies. Its Hispanic Leadership Development Program, for example, gives board and management training to leaders of Hispanic agencies.

To assertions that minorities are not adequately represented among United Way staffs and volunteer boards and committees, the United Way argues that United Ways have affirmative action programs. It lists 65 minorities and 134 women of the 231 people who have entered United Way careers from the United Way Management Training program. Fourteen and seven-tenths percent of United Way professionals are minorities. In United Ways across the country there were 2,934 women working in professional positions, including 306 chief professional officers.

Many alternative groups compete for workplace funding. In South Carolina the Other Way competes with the United Way. Also, health agency federations have competed with the United Way for workplace funding. In Rhode Island the Fund for Community Progress includes twenty agencies. It raised $180,000 in 1986, and it gained access to state employees following a lawsuit charging constitutional violations and was awarded $1,000 for damages.

Another challenge to the United Way occurred in the summer of 1986 in Los Angeles when the largest United Way in the nation was accused of the misuse of charitable contributions to pay for personal loans to top executives. *Los Angeles Times* reporter David Johnston, who like Kathleen Teltoch at the *New York Times*, covered news about philanthropy, lost his job after his front-page story about the scandal. Eventually the Los Angeles United Way president resigned. The Los Angeles United Way had had a 1987 goal of $90 million to serve 350 agencies, but the controversy made the goal hard to reach. Similarly, the Orange County United Way found it difficult to raise funds because of the overall challenge to United Way credibility.

Finally, various media have requested disclosure by United Way of its executive salaries. In late 1987 Congress approved a bill requiring all nonprofits to make their Form 990 tax returns available at their main offices. Thus, the public will be able to learn more about United Way budget items.

PERSONAL EXPERIENCES

I once worked for a United Way agency, Catholic Charities, in Houston as a maternity caseworker. All employees were encouraged to give to the United Way. When I was a contributions analyst at Pennzoil one of my projects was to contact Pennzoil offices around the country, including Pennzoil's mining and refinery locations, regarding their United Way contributions. Next I served for three years on a budget committee of Tulsa's United Way, deciding each year whether to approve the budget requests of four social service agencies. Tulsa United Way requested that we not disclose information about our committee's work. Also I have worked for a law firm that encouraged contributions to the United Way, and I teach at Oral Roberts University, another contributor to the United Way. My "Successful Fund Raising" class has hosted the local campaign coordinators and one trainee as guest speakers. It will be interesting to watch how United Way meets its many challenges.

RESUMÉ OF A UNITED WAY EXECUTIVE

WILLIAM ARAMONY
PRESIDENT
UNITED WAY OF AMERICA

Principal Current Position

May 18, 1970	-	Appointed President of United Way of America and President, United Way International
May 1964 to May 1970	-	Executive Director, United Fund of Dade County, Miami, Florida
June 1961 to May 1964	-	Executive Director, United Community Services of St. Joseph County, Inc., South Bend, Indiana

Other Current Affiliations

- Secretary-General, International Council on United Fund Raising
- Vice President, International Standing Conference on Philanthropy (INTERPHIL)
- Member, Board of Trustees, Clark University
- Member, Board of Directors and Management Committee, Independent Sector
- Member, Board of Trustees, Mutual of America
- Member, Board of Trustees, University of Notre Dame

United Way of America Programs and Services Created Under William Aramony's Leadership

1972	National headquarters relocated from New York City to Alexandria, Virginia, to better address the needs of United Ways and the voluntary sector. Government-relations activities upgraded to better shape Congressional legislation and programs affecting the delivery of human services around the country. National Academy for Voluntarism established to offer a variety of training programs for United Ways and other not-for-profit organizations.
1972	United Way became the standardized name for affiliated organizations throughout the nation. The creation of a standard logo and symbol--the familiar hand and rainbow--symbolized the United Way movement's ability to bring hope to people in need.
1973	"Standards of Excellence" developed to offer United Ways guidelines, operating principles and objectives, and benchmarks to measure their performance.
1974	National Football League began a relationship with United Way, to provide the nation's largest television and radio public-service campaign.
1976	National Corporate Development program created to increase employee's understanding of and commitment to United Way.

More than 300 of the nation's major corporations—representing 13 million employees—now participate.

Strategic Planning process established to help United Ways more effectively address rapidly changing social conditions. A Strategic Planning volunteer committee, made up of some of the nation's top futurists, continues to help United Ways and voluntary organizations anticipate and plan for the future.

1982   National Service Center opened at national headquarters to increase United Way of America's ability to assist and support professionals and volunteers from local United Ways and other health and human-service agencies. Training programs offered include management, communications, community problem solving and fund raising. A film and television studio produces the annual National Football League public service messages and multimedia programs for United Ways, and develops materials for other nonprofit organizations as well.

1983   Project Flagship, a microcomputer database system, developed to help United Ways organize, evaluate, process, and share information. Use of this database makes community health and human-care planning more efficient and effective.

1983   Gifts In Kind program initiated to supplement financial support for nonprofit organizations. Products, goods, and services are donated by America's corporations.

1985   Rethinking Tomorrow and Beyond written to provide United Ways with a strategic direction as they prepare for their second century of service, beginning in 1987. The document is based on a two-year exchange of ideas between local and national United Way leaders.

1985   Management training workshops and new research software developed to help United Ways train volunteers and share up-to-date information; MANAGE, BoardWALK, and Main Street are three products that have emerged from these efforts.

Education

1949   Clark University: bachelor's degree in business administration

1951   Boston College Graduate School of Social Work: master's degree in Social Work, Community Organization

Honors

Mr. Aramony has also received honorary degrees in humanities, humane letters, and doctor of laws.

Personal

Married and has three children.

6

Religious Fund Raising

INTRODUCTION

According to the Yankelovich, Skelly and White, Inc., study of charitable behavior, religious organizations receive the most individual contributions. Religious organizations received 72% of the contributions from the individuals in the study, and they received 85% of the contributions from the widowed, individuals over age sixty-five, individuals with less than a high school education, and individuals who attend church weekly or nearly weekly (White 1986:2). The study also ranked the types of organizations that receive gifts because of the donor's religious convictions: (1) charities that assist the poor, (2) organizations that help the poor internationally, (3) medical charities, and (4) educational institutions. In addition, those donors who contribute to a church or synagogue are more likely to contribute to a nonreligious organization than people who do not donate to a church or synagogue. In fact, the donors who give the greatest percentage of their income to philanthropy, as high as 3% of their income or more, also give a larger percentage of their total gifts to religious causes than do peopole who donate a smaller percentage of their income overall. Those who give a large percentage (3% or more) of incomes under $20,000 give 81% of their gifts to religious causes, compared to 72% of the gifts of middle-level givers and 57% of low-level givers. Similarly, those who give 3% or more of incomes between $20,000 and $40,000 give 80% of their donations to religious causes, compared to 58% of the gifts of middle-level givers and 61% of the gifts of low-level givers in the same income bracket. Of those with incomes of $40,000 or more, 69% of the contributions of those who give 3% or more of their income to philanthropy go to religious causes, compared to 54% of the gifts of middle-level givers and 54% of low-level givers. Also, there is a positive correlation between regular church attendance and the giving of greater percentages of income to religious organizations (White 1986:4–6).

Thus, religion is a vital part of philanthropy. In fact, the future of philanthropy in this country is tied to the future of religion here. It would be harmful for United States religion to follow the path of religion in Western Europe, leading to state-controlled philanthropy. As it is, there are several types of religious fund raising, including churches, denominational governing bodies, interdenominational organizations, and evangelical ministries. Although there is debate about the distinction between these types, the IRS simply distinguishes between "churches" and other nonprofit organizations.

People give to people in religious organizations too. Church leaders or ministers are obviously key individuals for church contributions. In turn, church contributions go to denominational governing bodies and to interdenominational organizations. These groups then disburse monies to various social service agencies and to missions. Similarly, evangelical ministries raise funds and then distribute them to various projects. The Evangelical Council for Financial Accountability (ECFA), endorses religious organizations that maintain certain ethical standards for fund raising.

CHURCHES

According to former IRS commissioner Jerome Kurtz's fourteen-point list of church characteristics, a "church" must have

1. A distinct legal existence
2. A recognized creed and form of worship

3. A definite and distinct ecclesiastical government

4. A formal code of doctrine and discipline

5. A distinct religious history

6. A membership not associated with any other church or denomination

7. A complete organization of ordained ministers ministering to their congregations

8. Ordained ministers selected after completing prescribed courses of study

9. A literature of its own

10. Established places of worship

11. Regular congregations

12. Regular religious services

13. Sunday schools for the religious instructions of the young

14. Schools for the preparation of its ministers

An organization meeting a preponderance of these items would be considered a "church" (*Ministries Today* 1986b:16).

The principle of "people give to people" applies in church giving. In the local church the pastor or priest is the key person. Many people shop around for a church, and their choice depends largely on the personality of the man or woman in the pulpit.

Most local churches collect offerings each Sunday. For Protestant churches the pastor's salary may come partly from money collected. The son-in-law of the late Smith Wigglesworth, a pastor in Britain, described one incident:

At one time the pastor of a very large church said to him: "Brother, you have been here three months and your ministry has put this work on a new and solid footing. You cannot leave us. Our people have demanded that we retain you at any price, and the board of this church has asked me to request you to name your figure. You can have anything you want if you will only stay with us." The speaker went on to suggest an astronomical amount if he would only continue his ministry in that church, but Wigglesworth was adamant as he replied: "I have done what God wanted me to do in this place, and now not all the money in the world would be enough to keep me. Gather your church board together and I will pray with you and them, and then say good-bye." A pleading, weeping group of men met him and urged him to reconsider his verdict, but he had made up his mind. He prayed with them and for them and left them saying: "I have a peace no money can buy. I have heaven's smile, and that is worth millions of dollars. I have the divine approval that I would not sacrifice for all the gold in the world. A minute under the unction of God is worth more than worlds. The good will of God on my head and heart is priceless treasure. Should I sacrifice these for earth's gold? Never!! Never!!" (Frodsham 1948:132, copyright Gospel Publishing House, reprinted by permission.)

Pastors use a variety of methods to encourage their congregations to give offerings to the church. For example, Tulsa's First Christian Church bulletin of November 1, 1981, carried the following announcement:

TODAY MARKS THE OPENING DAY OF THE PONY EXPRESS RUN: Welcome the member of First Christian that brings the saddle bag to your home. After completing your estimate of giving card, take the saddle bag on to the next member of the saddle bag list. Do your part to help FCC reach a "Breakthrough in '82" by underwriting the budget of $603,670.

Pastor Jim Sanderson of First Baptist Church of Jenks, Oklahoma, wrote in the church's October 8, 1985, newsletter:

September was a difficult month for us financially (September always is). Being a five Sunday month that has Labor Day (one of our weakest days for the year) made it all doubly difficult this year. Usually our income is not greater on five Sunday months as over against four Sunday months. But our budget requirements are greater. This last month we fell behind our budget needs by $4,000.

I am not panicked . . . yet! October through December is one of our better quarters. Join me in cleaning up the budget deficit by the end of this month. Then let us be far ahead of our budget needs by the end of December.

Churches have raised record offerings in a single day. In 1983 a Church of Christ in Texas held the record by raising $2.2 million. Second place was held by a Christian Church in Washington state with $1.7 million. The Tulsa Garnett Church of Christ raised over $1.5 million in one day in 1983 for its new church sanctuary.

Robert Schuller's Crystal Cathedral in Garden Grove, California, once raised $1.4 million.

Most churches eventually use their offerings to build new buildings. A Tulsa newspaper account of the Garnett Church of Christ's record $1.5 million offering stated that the church saved nearly $2 million in interest by not borrowing to pay for the construction of its new 3,500-seat sanctuary. However, the newspaper reported that some members borrowed to make their offering, such as one unemployed church member who borrowed $1,000 from a Tulsa bank on a program, arranged by church elders, in which the church underwrote such loans. Members borrowed a total of $554,755 from the bank to donate to the offering for the new sanctuary. Specific items included in the Garnett Church of Christ's record offering included several vintage automobiles and two motorcycles. At least five women gave diamond rings, including wedding rings. Some families sold their rental property and gave the money to the church, and others deeded rental property for the church elders to sell. The largest single gift was $63,000 in cash. There were small sacrificial gifts too. A boy gave the $10 he had received for his birthday. A mission congregation of sixty members in Augusta, Georgia, that was begun by the Garnett Church of Christ gave $1,105 from a collection they had taken a week earlier.

Church offerings are a routine dimension of religious fund raising. Church sanctuaries and other buildings are visible records of those offerings. Throughout history, though, people have been quick to criticize clergy who build ornate church buildings in centers of poverty. People have also criticized churches for taking certain offerings. The list of specific gifts in the Garnett church offering is illustrative. When some people hear that women gave even their wedding rings they may be critical of the church or the women. Here there is a need for more complete information. Would the critics be less critical if it turned out the women who gave their wedding rings were so wealthy that they were planning to buy bigger diamonds to replace them anyway? Also there is a difference in criticism if the boy's birthday gift came from a boy whose family was impoverished rather than from one whose parents had already established a sizeable trust fund for their son. Yet there is a Biblical response to the critics even if those gifts came from people in poverty. The New Testament widow who gave her last coins to the church is one example (Mark 12:41–44; Luke 21:4).

Another controversial issue is the concept of tithing, which originates in the Old Testament. Some churches teach that all members should give a tithe, or one-tenth of their incomes. Some churches even specify that the tenth should come from the members' gross incomes and not merely their net income. Among churches that encourage tithing, some also exhort their members to tithe to the church and not to various evangelical ministries that they do not consider to be "churches."

Another controversial dimension of religious fund raising is the concept of "seed-faith." Oral Roberts has popularized the concept, and many local church ministers use it. The "seed-faith" concept is that giving is a natural part of life in response to God's gift to us of His Son, Jesus. Therefore, each person ought to be continually giving time, talents, money, etc., and ought to expect a harvest from the planting of such "seed" to meet his need.

Billy Joe Daugherty is the pastor of a large and fast-growing church in Tulsa, Oklahoma. One of the reasons for the growth of his church has to do with giving. The following is an interview with him:

REPORTER: As a minister of a large church in Tulsa, Oklahoma, what are your views on giving? When did you start to give?

REV. DAUGHERTY: When I was 10 years old God started dealing with my heart on giving. I started to mow lawns and begin to give part of the money I earned. When I did, I had some of my own needs met. I learned from experience that giving to God is never a loss. It's always an investment.

REPORTER: Isn't 10 years old a young age to start giving?

REV. DAUGHERTY: No. I think when we teach our children about giving, they have no problem with it. Too often without knowing it we instruct them in selfishness and greed.

REPORTER: How do you teach your own children to give?

REV. DAUGHERTY: Our children are very young, so we teach them to give their toys away or their clothes. We have *them* give them away. This way, they learn the joy of giving and they see miracles, too. We point out to them that the things they receive come back to them *through* a person, but they are given to them by God.

REPORTER: How has your giving changed since you were a child?

REV. DAUGHERTY: Today, *everything* I have belongs to God. I am a steward of what God has entrusted me with. That includes my money, my talents and time, my children. So when I give, I am acknowledging that I belong to God and that God is responsible for my welfare.

REPORTER: What about people who are afraid to give because they won't have enough to pay the rent and other bills? How do you help them?

REV. DAUGHERTY: The key is the scriptures. Romans 10:17 says, "Faith comes by hearing the Word." The more we study the Word, the more faith we have. And faith replaces fear. When faith comes, we do what we do out of obedience to the Word. Out of this obedience to the Word comes cheerfulness and joy.

REPORTER: What do you tell people who have given and seem to have no return?

REV. DAUGHERTY: Again the key is scripture. The Bible teaches a time of endurance and perseverance. To continue doing His will *until* we obtain the promise. Hebrews 10:35 says, "Cast not away your confidence which hath great recompense of reward. For you have need of patience, that after you have done the will of God, you might receive the promise." Galatians 6:9 tells us, "Don't quit giving. In due time you *will* reap." God's Word never fails. If there is a failure somewhere, it's not God who is at fault. If we can't trust God, there isn't anybody better than Him to trust.

REPORTER: With the economy so shaky do you feel people should continue giving?

REV. DAUGHERTY: I encourage people to seek the kingdom first. Sometimes I say, "I wish everybody here would stop working for a living." I didn't say stop working. But stop working for a *living*. Work for God and He will provide your living. Seek the kingdom first . . . put God and His work first. When we do that, we are promised that everything we need will be added to us . . . not subtracted.

REPORTER: How do you feel about Seed-Faith?

REV. DAUGHERTY: Seed-Faith is a way of directing what we do toward God and believing that He will multiply it back. Jesus taught Seed-Faith. If you read the rest of Matthew 6:33 it says, "If you will seek the kingdom first, all these things will be added unto you." What is that? That's Seed-Faith. Jesus was saying don't seek the things of the world . . . lands, houses, riches. Don't make them your priority. That's what the Gentiles do. Seek the kingdom first, and you will have all those things given to you by God. You won't need to *seek* for them or to struggle and work for those things. People who really do practice Seed-Faith live an abundant, prosperous life that is the envy of those who don't practice it.

REPORTER: When a person lives in poverty should he give to the gospel?

REV. DAUGHERTY: Yes. Seed-Faith is the cure for that poverty. It cures the rich man's greed and the poor man's poverty. It cures both extremes and brings balance.

REPORTER: Didn't Jesus direct His disciples to live in poverty when He sent them out without any money or food or a change of clothing?

REV. DAUGHERTY: No. If you read on, Jesus says to them later, "Do you remember when I sent you out without anything? Did you lack anything?" That was the key. Jesus was teaching them *total dependence and trust in God . . . not poverty.*

REPORTER: How can a person in today's world get to the place where he is willing to be totally dependent on God?

REV. DAUGHERTY: By giving. When you sow seed, you put yourself in a position where you've *got to have* miracles. If a person doesn't believe in Seed-Faith, he holds on to his money and he never grows. His giving habits are a measure of his spiritual growth and maturity. When you give, you prosper in mind, body, family, finances, and social life. This is the whole person concept and that's God's plan.

REPORTER: Do you see this happening today in the Church?

REV. DAUGHERTY: Yes. The Church is rising to the top in every realm: in technology, business, media, and in government. Praise God! We have a Christian President today. Christian education is also coming in like a flood. God is raising up the Church in the last days through the Seed-Faith principle.

REPORTER: What do you think about your church people giving part of their tithe to other ministries?

REV. DAUGHERTY: First, we must define what the Church is. The Church is the redeemed. Who are its leaders? The apostle, the prophet, the evangelist, the pastor, and the teacher. These are the five types of leaders . . . carrying out the five-fold ministry. The Church is all the Christians everywhere. That includes Methodists, Baptists, the Full Gospel Businessmen, Oral Roberts, his partners, and others . . . that's what the Church is. Scripture says to bring the tithe into the storehouse. There is a storehouse in the apostolic ministry, the evangelistic ministry, and the other church ministries. All of these bring forth food to the people of God for nourishment and upbuilding of the Body of Christ. We never discourage our people from giving into other ministries.

We as a church have not suffered any loss by our people giving to other ministries because our people's needs have been met. Our vision for the total ministry of Christ is larger than our structure here—our four walls. We as a local church give to ministries and missions around the world. When people bring money into the storehouse—our church for instance—people have brought it into the storehouse trusting us to be a *channel* to where it's needed. We can't do everything as a local church, and we are not just interested in building up our group and nothing else. We are interested in reaching the world for Jesus, and so we assist those who are doing the work we are not doing by giving to them.

REPORTER: What do you see as the key to a church's financial problems?

REV. DAUGHERTY: There are several keys to solving churches' financial problems. First is seeing God as the Source of all things needed in this life. Second is the aspect of giving as a seed. Churches can give just like individuals. Third is expecting God to multiply the seed sown.

All of this may sound familiar, but it really is not an Oral Roberts principle. Seed-Faith is God's principle that Brother Roberts discovered and put into practice.

REPORTER: How do you feel the Oral Roberts Ministries manages the money given into it?

REV. DAUGHERTY: I think they do a good job. People who plant seed in the Oral Roberts Ministries have the joy of knowing they have planted seed in fertile soil. The seed that has been planted has been used to minister to people. The money is used to support radio and TV programs that minister to people, to build a university that trains students to go out and minister. People channel their funds there because they see someone doing what they can't do on their own. ("A Pastor Speaks Out On Giving" from *Abundant Life Magazine* 1983, Copyright © 1983 by Oral Roberts Evangelistic Association, reprinted by permission of Oral Roberts Evangelistic Association.)

Church fund raising involves other issues too. Should churches use offering envelopes? Should they give each member a record of his total gifts for IRS purposes? Once the offering is collected, there is the issue of who should count the money collected. Should more than one person count it? Should the same person deposit it in the bank? How is confidentiality maintained regarding personal checks?

One Tulsa church had the disillusioning experience of having a pastor leave town without any warning except for a notice on the closed church doors. Affluent members of the church had unwisely backed church debts, and they were left personally indebted when the pastor fled. That pastor had been a guest speaker in my fund raising class, recommended by one of the students. A few of the students saw the dangers in his church policies during his presentation. Part of the students' grade in my course is a brief written evaluation of each guest speaker, and we also discuss the presentation without the guest speaker present. In the case of that particular pastor, a few of the students expressed serious concern about his autocratic control of church finances after he had described his rather paranoid procedures for securing all church funds. He had little or no business background, and the church's financial situation was disastrous, but he apparently did not submit the problem to his church members.

There can be power struggles in churches too. Some churches have a tendency to appoint members as lay leaders simply because they are the biggest contributors to the church budget. The use of pledges for church budgets provides a preview of which members plan to give the most. (Churches may allow a cushion of approximately 7% to cover unfulfilled pledges.) Those members who are big contributors may exert undue influence to control the church budget process. They may compete with the pastor regarding church budget decisions. An example of a church that has a budget of over $1 million and that tries to guarantee diverse input in its budget process is First United Methodist of Tulsa:

Each year every department in the church takes a good survey of its budget expenditures (about November). This gives them a chance to evaluate what they have been doing during the year, and to see the actual cost involved in getting it done. Then each department head must immediately begin setting up his or her budget for the coming year. While the experience of prior years helps them in doing this, each year is started on a "zero" budget basis. Some prior programs are continued, some are dropped, and some new ones are worked in. All of this is carefully evaluated and costed out by the department head.

In early January all of these budgets are thoroughly discussed with the pastor and senior minister by the department heads. Then soon after that sessions are set up involving all of the ministers and all of the department heads in relating the proposed budgets to the potential cash that will be available. After this is completed then a long evening session is set up with the Finance Committee executive group. Following this the total budget is presented to the total Finance Committee and then, following that, it is presented to the full Administrative Board. All of these sessions are open for full challenges and questions from all of the people involved. The result is that the budget has been very well evaluated by the time the Administrative Board has finally approved it. (Membership brochure)

Another issue is how much detailed information about the budget to provide to all church members and how often. Should the budget be in the weekly church bulletin? Should pastoral and staff salary amounts be specified?

Nonprofit agencies may apply to churches to receive allocations from the church budget. Representatives of the agency should apply for funds according to whatever procedure the church has established. Representatives will probably need to present a written proposal for funds, and they will probably meet with members of the church budget committee and possibly with other leaders in the church, including the pastor. There is, therefore, another "people give to people" aspect in church fund raising. The best agency representatives to solicit the church for funds will be church members, preferably in leadership positions on the agency board.

Occasionally a church budget will include a category such as "missions" or "outreach." Agency representatives should learn what amount may be available to them through that budget category. For example, St. Luke's Methodist in Houston has annually given five different agencies or organizations gifts of $25,000 each. The A.D. Players was a recipient of such a gift. A group of board members from the A.D. Players presented a desktop slide presentation in the office of one of the church members who served on the committee to select the agencies that would receive the $25,000 gifts. Also, another church member who was very involved with A.D. Players fund raising informed the Players of the availability of the contribution.

DENOMINATIONAL AND
INTERDENOMINATIONAL FUNDING

Another dimension of church funding involves regional and national denominational governing bodies. Different denominations have different names for their governing bodies, for example, "Presbytery" for the Presbyterian church. Some denominations use a formula wherein each church gives according to the size of its membership and the total church budget. If there is not a specific formula, there will be a "people give to people" aspect when a representative of the governing body negotiates with the church pastor about the church's contributions. The denominational bodies will, in turn, distribute part of the money to "outreach" programs, etc.

Besides denominational giving, there is also interdenominational giving. Many communities have metropolitan or urban ministries similar to the United Way that centralize funding from many different churches. Nationally there is the National Council of Churches. The World Council of Churches is the international interdenomination organization. These larger interdenominational organizations generally collect funds from the denominational governing bodies. Once again interpersonal factors are important as representatives of the interdenominational organizations send representatives to meet with the denominations.

The disbursement of interdenominational funds has been controversial. The World Council of Churches has been criticized for allegedly funding guerrilla activities in countries such as Rhodesia. Some churches have refused to give their funds to interdenominational organizations for use in military activities. Some may refuse to give to military activities that they consider left-wing, and some may refuse to sponsor what they perceive as right-wing activities. Sometimes it is difficult to follow funds given internationally all the way to their final destination. If the money is spent for food, for example, warring factions within the country may consider the funds politically tainted even if they only feed orphans from the opposing faction. U.S. church members may prefer to give food gifts instead of weapons, but the food gifts may indirectly provide those in the recipient country with weapons, bought with money not needed for food.

EVANGELICAL MINISTRIES

Evangelical ministries, particularly the televangelists, received intense media coverage in 1987, and the House Ways and Means Oversight Subcommittee began to investigate the major televangelistic organizations' tax-exempt status. Most evangelical ministries would not generally be considered "churches," although some actually have their own churches. For those of their contributors who tithe, whether or not the ministry is a church is significant: those contributers may choose to give their tithe to their local church, leaving only offerings above and beyond the tithe for other ministries.

Evangelical ministries include traditional missionary programs. There are also radio outreaches. The 1,200-member National Religious Broadcasters Association reports that there are 1,370 radio stations with religious formats and 221 television stations dedicated to religion. Evangelical ministries also involve outreaches such as an accredited university, a teaching hospital, a cable network, and an amusement park.

The morality and lifestyles of evangelical leaders must be beyond reproach to maintain contributions. Moreover, their stewardship of the finances entrusted to them should meet a high fiduciary standard. The finances involved are many millions of dollars.

There is a dilemma, though, as evangelists make daily decisions about what clothes to wear, what house to buy, etc. The television evangelists especially face the temptation of imitating Hollywood lifestyles. They may be afraid of losing part of their audience if they are less "showy."

Even before the creation of the fictional Elmer Gantry, cynics accused evangelists of being charlatans. Attorneys representing disillusioned contributors in lawsuits against evangelical ministries and churches use arguments such as fraud in the inducement, breach of contract, and undue influence in their cases. One way to help distinguish the actual from the perceived misuse of funds is for all evangelical ministries to publish the salaries of all top executives, as well as such donations as real estate and houses. Annual reports of all income and expenditures would allow contributors to make better decisions about which evangelists to support.

People give to people in evangelical ministries too. The founding

personality or top executive is the primary fund raiser, although
evangelical organizations may hire various development officers.
Certainly the change of the PTL ministry leadership from the Bak-
kers to Jerry Falwell meant contributors would give only if they
approved the new leadership, and they would likewise need to
approve other leaders following Jerry Falwell's resignation.

One controversy surrounding evangelical ministries is the methods they use to solicit donations. On television or through direct
mail they may claim an emergency situation. Guidance for contributors to evangelical ministries may be given in the story of the
prophet Elijah's request of the starving widow of Zarephath that
she give him some bread—analogous to asking one of the tragic
famine mothers in Ethiopia for food. Elijah finally convinced her
to feed him, claiming that there would be a miraculous replenish-
ing of her food supply, but it is important to note that God had
commanded her to feed Elijah before Elijah even made the request
(I Kings 17:8–16).

Not all donations to evangelical ministries come from people of
like-minded religious persuasion. Thus, there is the issue of whether
any nonprofit organization should accept contributions from donors who are ideologically divergent from the organization. Oral
Roberts' ministries received a gift of over $1 million from a Flor-
ida man who had made his money in dog racing. His gift is an
exception to the idea that "people give to people," unless a member of the Oral Roberts' ministries personally solicited him. Media
accounts said he merely gave because of his belief in education.

The solution to all emergency appeals is full disclosure. What is
the exact budget of the project? What is the long-term plan for
funding the project? How will contributions in excess of the requested amount be used? Of course, there should be no "bait and
switch" technique of requesting funds for one project and using
them for something else.

Offering premiums is another method evangelical ministries use
as an inducement to contributors. Premiums are gift items given
for contributions. It would help contributors figure their IRS deductions if the evangelical ministries told them the value of the
premiums.

EVANGELICAL COUNCIL FOR FINANCIAL ACCOUNTABILITY

In 1979, representatives from several major evangelistic organizations met with lawyers and CPAs who specialized in nonprofit organizations and formed the Evangelical Council for Financial Accountability. The organization has headquarters at 2915 Hunter Mill Road, Suite 17, P.O. Box 659, Oakton, VA 22124, 703-938-6006. Its mission is "to develop, promote and enforce the highest standards of financial integrity and accountability among its evangelical constituency."

The president of ECFA is Arthur C. Borden. Mr. Borden worked for twenty-five years with an international ministry, and he worked with federal agencies and the U.S. Congress serving the government of Puerto Rico. He was also liaison to U.S. denominations and churches for the American Bible Society. The ECFA board members include representatives of the Billy Graham Evangelistic Association, Campus Crusade for Christ, Fuller Theological Seminary, Moody Bible Institute of Chicago, John Brown University, Navigators, Taylor University, the Baptist General Conference, and World Vision.

In 1986, ECFA membership increased 8% from 315 to 341 members. Members have a cumulative donor income of over $1.18 billion. Over $40 billion was given to U.S. churches and other religious organizations in 1986, with ECFA members getting 2.75%.

An ECFA goal is to meet its operating expenses from member fees. In 1986 it was within 10% of that goal, and the balance of its expenses were covered by gifts from individuals, foundations, and other organizations. In 1986 ECFA income was $307,646, and expenses were $285,718, with 65.4% for programs, 30% administrative, and 4.6% fund raising. The member fees are based on total cash contributions the member receives, not in-kind contributions, and the total fee is prorated on a monthly basis. The fees range from $175 for evangelical organizations with incomes up to $250,000, to $500,000 for organizations with cash contributions over $50 million. Of the 341 members, 27% have incomes in the lowest range and provide 8% of ECFA's member fees and receive 1% of the contributions that members receive from donors. Seventeen and nine-tenths percent of members have incomes between $250,000 and $500,000, 14.4% have incomes between $500,000 and $1 million, 14.4% have incomes between $1 million and $2 million, 14.4% have incomes between $2 million and $5 million, and 5.9% have incomes between $5 million and $10 million. Six and two-tenths percent have incomes of $10 million or more and provide 33% of member fees and receive 64% of contributions from donors.

Organizations interested in becoming members must complete an application form. Acceptance as members allows the organization to use the ECFA seal as long as the organization continues to have a good faith compliance with ECFA standards. The standards include a doctrinal statement of faith provided either by the member or the ECFA Statement of Faith:

1. We believe the Bible to be the inspired, the only infallible, authoritative Word of God.

2. We believe that there is one God, eternally existent in three persons: Father, Son, and Holy Spirit.

3. We believe in the deity of Christ, in His virgin birth, in His sinless life, in His miracles, in His vicarious and atoning death through His shed blood, in His bodily resurrection, in His ascension to the right hand of the Father, and in His personal return in power and glory.

4. We believe that for the salvation of lost and sinful men regeneration by the Holy Spirit is absolutely essential.

5. We believe in the present ministry of the Holy Spirit, by whose indwelling the Christian is enabled to live a godly life.

6. We believe in the resurrection of both the saved and the lost, they that are saved unto the resurrection of life and they that are lost unto the resurrection of damnation.

7. We believe in the spiritual unity of believers in our Lord Jesus Christ.

The organization must also show that it has a responsible Board of Directors. The majority of board members may not be employees/staff and/or related by blood or marriage. The board must meet at least semi-annually. The board must have general responsibility for reviewing and establishing the programs and policies of the organization, including adopting the annual budget in advance and overseeing it or providing an explanation if it does not. The board should determine the CEO's annual compensation, or it should explain why it does not.

Members must submit an annual audit by an independent public accounting firm using GASS and GAAP, generally accepted auditing standards and procedures. The audit should include all subsidiary and affiliate programs, or the organization must provide an explanation. The organization must also determine what percentages of its expenses are used for fund raising, management, and program. There must be an audit review committee to review the audit and report to the board, with a majority of the committee not employees/staff and/or related by blood or marriage.

Applicants must explain any conflicts of interest wherein board or staff members or their families have a financial interest in or receive compensation from any firm or organization conducting business with the organization. The applicants must also explain any investigations by government authorities or any litigation they are involved in. They must explain failure to comply with all laws relating to financial reporting and disclosure, charitable solicitation laws, security regulations, and other statutory provisions.

Finally, the organization must comply with ECFA Standards for Fund Raising:

1. TRUTHFULNESS IN COMMUNICATION:
   All representations of fact, description of financial condition of the organization, or narrative about events must be current, complete and accurate. References to past activities or events must be appropriately dated. There must be no material omissions or exaggerations of fact or use of misleading photographs or any other communication which would tend to create a false impression or misunderstanding.

2. COMMUNICATION AND DONOR EXPECTATIONS:
   Fund raising appeals must not create unrealistic donor expectations of what a donor's gift will actually accomplish within the limits of the organization's ministry.

3. COMMUNICATION AND DONOR INTENT:
   All statements made by the organization in its fund raising appeals about the use of the gift must be honored by the organization. The donor's intent is related to both what was communicated in the appeal and to any donor instructions accompanying the gift. The organization should be aware that communications made in fund raising appeals may create a legally binding restriction.

4. PROJECTS UNRELATED TO A MINISTRY'S PRIMARY PUR-
POSE:
An organization raising or receiving funds for programs that are not
part of its present or prospective ministry, but are proper in accordance with its exempt purpose, must either treat them as restricted
funds and channel them through an organization that can carry out
the donor's intent, or return the funds to the donor.

5. INCENTIVES AND PREMIUMS:
Fund raising appeals which, in exchange for a contribution, offer
premiums or incentives (the value of which is not insubstantial, but
which is significant in relation to the amount of the donation) must
advise the donor, both in the solicitation and in the receipt, of the
fair market value of the premium or incentive and that the value is
not deductible for tax purposes.

6. REPORTING:
An organization must provide, on request, a report, including financial information, on the project for which it is soliciting gifts.

7. PERCENTAGE COMPENSATION FOR FUND RAISERS:
Compensation of outside fund raising consultants based directly or
indirectly on a percentage of what is raised, or on any other contingency agreement, may create potential conflicts and opportunities for
abuse. Full disclosure of such arrangements is required, at least annually, in the organization's audited financial statements, in which
the disclosure must match income and related expenses. Compensation to the organization's own employees on a percentage basis or
contingency basis is not allowed.

8. TAX DEDUCTIBLE GIFTS FOR A NAMED RECIPIENT'S PER-
SONAL BENEFIT:
Tax deductible gifts may not be used to pass money or benefits to
any named individual for personal use.

9. CONFLICT OF INTEREST ON ROYALTIES:
An officer, director, or other principal of the organization must not
receive royalties for any product that is used for fund raising or pro-
motional purposes by his/her own organization.

10. ACKNOWLEDGMENT OF GIFTS IN KIND:
Property or gifts in kind received by an organization, should be acknowledged describing the property or gift accurately *without* a
statement of the gift's market value. It is the responsibility of the
donor to determine the fair market value of the property for tax
purposes. But the organization should inform the donor of IRS reporting requirements for all gifts in excess of $5,000.

11. ACTING IN THE INTEREST OF THE DONOR:
    An organization must make every effort to avoid accepting a gift from or entering into a contract with a prospective donor which would knowingly place a hardship on the donor, or place the donor's future well-being in jeopardy.

12. FINANCIAL ADVICE:
    The representative of the organization, when dealing with persons regarding commitments on major estate assets, must seek to guide and advise donors so they have adequately considered the broad interests of the family and the various ministries they are currently supporting before they make a final decision. Donors should be encouraged to use the services of their attorneys, accountants, or other professional advisors. (ECFA 1986:2)

ECFA has considered expanding some of its requirements. One suggestion is that members not only accept a doctrinal statement of faith but also comply with it in their operations. Another suggestion is that members demonstrate financial integrity by such actions as current payment to creditors in accordance with agreed-upon terms, documentation of all borrowing with repayment authorized by the board, normal operation in the black, adequate management controls over the disbursement of funds, and a description of any litigation that could affect the financial well-being of the organization.

ECFA has compliance review procedures that include some due process. A Review Team carries out the review of members allegedly out of compliance. In 1986 twenty ECFA members dealt with compliance issues, and one organization faced a major review, but it was found to be in compliance.

Through its activities, ECFA hopes to help avoid excessive government restrictions of nonprofit organizations. It also wants to assure all donors of their rights to:

1. Know how the funds of an organization are being spent.

2. Know what the programs are accomplishing.

3. Know that the organization is in compliance with federal, state, and municipal laws.

4. Restrict or designate gifts to a particular project.

5. Receive a response to inquiries about finances and programs.

6. Visit offices and program sites of an organization to talk personally with the staff.

7. Not be pressured into giving to any organization.

8. Know that the organization is well managed.

9. Know that there is a responsible governing board and know who those board members are.

10. Know that all appeals for funds are truthful and accurate.

PERSONAL EXPERIENCES

During my graduate studies in social work at the University of Texas I had a one-semester, full-time field placement at Austin Presbyterian Theological Seminary where I observed seminarians eager to be hired by affluent churches. I also worked with the United Urban Council, a metropolitan ministries program of several Austin denominations. There I served on various committees while the council endeavored to decide where to allocate its funds: the Research and Planning Division, Current Program Division, and Economic Resources Division. I also helped to organize the Hispanic Community Development Task Force. The task force successfully requested funding for a day-care center for El Buen Pastor United Methodist Church and for the El Centro de la Gente de Aztlan in the barrio of East Austin. In addition, I assisted in the evaluation of other grant applications for the council.

Another personal experience with religious philanthropy was my work with the After Dinner (A.D.) Players, a Christian theatre company in Houston. It was natural for the A.D. Players to seek funding from churches. During that time the company received $25,000 from St. Luke's United Methodist Church after requesting funds through the church's special committee.

As a faculty member at Oral Roberts University I have observed fund raising for the ministry. The ORU Development Office, once known as the "Projects" office, has evolved from the one-man office of Dick Crawford, who later became Tulsa's mayor, to a well-staffed office with experienced fund raisers, and back to a one-woman office. During the period of full staffing, I declined an offer to work in the Development Office. However, I would like to see my students work in the Development Office because I believe alumni of any university are its most persuasive fund raisers. It is noteworthy that a 1982 survey by the Council for Advancement and Support of Education found that the average tenure of an advancement professional is less than three years (CASE 1983:1).

As the wife of an ORU medical student I have also observed Oral Roberts' medical fund raising. I am enthusiastic about medical missions, having been a teen volunteer in the Amigos de las Americas program in villages in Honduras and Guatemala and having worked in surgery and a ward in a German village hospital during college. The attempt by ORU to give medical school loans in exchange for work in medical missions is unique among medical schools.

My husband and I attended Tulsa's Victory Christian Center one Sunday when the pastor's wife gave a gold watch, valued at over $2,000, to the church building fund. The watch was a gift to her from a woman whose husband had been healed after the pastor had prayed for him in their home. The pastor's wife said that when she receives such gifts she explains to the givers that she may give their gifts away.

I had a roommate who grew up in Japan, where her parents were Baptist missionaries. Her mother, the daughter of an Alabama governor, exchanged her bubble bath lifestyle for life in a Japanese fishing village shortly after World War II. Later she became an administrator of a Christian university in Tokyo. Her daughter told me that her mother was criticized by other women in her denomination because they considered her clothes too fancy for a missionary. Yet, according to her daughter, her mother's clothes came from the same boxes of donated used clothing as did the other missionary wives' clothes. From her background, though, her mother simply knew how to wear clothes that would be the most becoming to her.

There was also a student in my fund raising class whose in-laws have a large televangelism ministry in Canada. The student told the class that her mother-in-law turned her rings so that the diamonds would not show. Her mother-in-law had inherited those rings, but she did not want to be criticized for wearing extravagant jewelry.

A guest speaker in my fund raising class one year was a man with an evangelistic outreach in Africa. The students criticized his expensive-looking gold watch and other jewelry. They did not challenge him directly, however, and the less-skeptical agreed that perhaps the jewelry had been gifts to him. Later a local television reporter won a national investigative reporting award for his story about that evangelist's questionable use of funds for such things as an airplane.

I visited Israel with televangelist Zola Levitt. In one newsletter he wrote:

First of all, I recently received a letter asking if I live in a mansion and wear a Rolex watch. In fact, my house is a typical middle-class, 3-bed-room brick in a Jewish neighborhood. I bought it to get a chance to witness to my people and it has worked. It cost me $33,000 in 1974. I paid for it personally, by the way, not the ministry. We have no housing allowances, car allowances, or expense accounts of any kind at Zola Lev-itt Ministries. You've read about a large ministry's "debtload" of 50 million dollars. Our debt load is zero.

If I could afford a Rolex watch I'd buy a newer car instead. I drive a '65 Buick by preference, but I have a '73 model also. My watch is the bottom-of-the-line Casio ($39.95).

The whole point here is just this: with an 11-person ministry working out of rented office space you sure don't have to worry about your money being wasted. On the contrary, stewardship that allows this handful of cheerful Christian workers to serve a million television viewers per week is nothing short of a miracle! And our program won the New York Film and Television Festival Award in two consecutive years.

We are not like the big ministries—we merely share the same medium, television. Please use your discernment. (Levitt 1987:1)

I have also observed Catholic ministries that have simple life-styles. As a maternity social worker at Catholic Charities I was a guest speaker at a Catholic high school in Beaumont, Texas, and I spent the night at the convent with the nuns there who run the school. The nuns did not wear habits, and I was surprised that one of the younger nuns had a white French poodle. Yet, their dormitory life was simple. I also helped with a mini-documentary about a German priest who was translating the Bible at the Pa-pago Indian reservation in Arizona. His lifestyle there appeared simple too.

During graduate school I lived for one year at "The Vine," a small, women's household of "The Well," a Christian community. I also interacted with households of Church of the Redeemer in Houston. Though I was never officially a member of either community I appreciated their efforts to emulate the communal lives of first-century Christians. However, I also saw the potential for such communities to become cults. One pessimistic theory is that all movements will inevitably become either organizations or cults.

My husband and I have attended Tulsa Chinese Christian Fellowship. There is no offering taken during the service. However, there is a box, where money may be given, near one of the church doors.

Even though "people give to people" in religious fund raising, there is a spiritual dimension to such giving. I am not a theologian, and I will leave it to the theologians to pursue the topic further. Religious funding is a vital part of philanthropy worthy of more scholarly research.

RESUMÉ OF A DENOMINATIONAL EXECUTIVE

HOWARD LEE PLOWMAN
Tulsa District Superintendent, United Methodist Church

BIRTHPLACE: Collinsville, Oklahoma

EDUCATION: Will Rogers High School, Tulsa, OK
                        University of Tulsa, Bachelor of Arts
                        Perkins School of Theology, Bachelor of Divinity

HONORS: Doctor of Divinity, Oklahoma City University

PASTORATES: Kellyville, Colbert-Calera, Tishomingo, Eighth
                        Street (Oklahoma City), Asbury (Ponca City), East
                        Cross (Bartlesville), Elk City, New Haven (Tulsa),
                        Ardmore First United Methodist (1978-1985).

CONFERENCE   Director of Conference Council on Ministries
APPOINTMENTS: 1973-1976
                        District Superintendent, Stillwater District 1976-
                        1978

CONFERENCE   Recent Chairman (1978-1984), Board of Global
RESPONSIBILITIES: Ministries, and past Chairman of Woodworth Estates
                        Committee which disburses $380,000 per year to
                        missionary projects. Past Chairman of Conference
                        Board of Christian Social Concerns, Vice President
                        of Conference Board of Evangelism. In past, served
                        as deans of camp, district work, etc. In 1979, led
                        conference campaign to raise $1,000,000 for Oklahoma
                        Methodist Manor Nursing building.

ECUMENICAL WORK: Vice President of Oklahoma Conference of Churches,
                        President of Central Oklahoma Multi-Media
                        Association, President of various ministerial
                        alliances.

COMMUNITY WORK: Presently, member of Downtown Rotary Club. Director
                        of Ardmore Rotary Club, Director of Kiwanis Club in
                        Bartlesville, member of Tulsa Chamber of Commerce,
                        member of Ardmore retirement center board, member of
                        Children's Shelter Board.

TELEVISION   Helped establish television ministry at First United
MINISTRY: Methodist Church of Ardmore, April, 1983.
                        Broadcasts weekly from the sanctuary--live worship
                        11:00 A.M. Sundays.

RESUMÉ OF A DENOMINATIONAL EXECUTIVE
(Cont.)

GENERAL
CHURCH
RESPONSIBILITIES:
Member of General Board of Church and Society for eight years (1972-1980). Member of 1976 and 1984 General Conference Delegation, First Alternate 1980. Member of Jurisdictional Conference Delegations 1972, 1976, 1980, 1984.

FAMILY:
Wife Trudy.
Children:
Donde Ashmos, Assistant Professor, University of Texas, Austin.
Sandra Kraus, New York City, N.Y.
Tom Plowman, completing his Masters of Business Administration, Oklahoma City University, Oklahoma City, OK

PUBLICATIONS:
Various articles for Church School Today, Crosstalk, and a lesson series for youth entitled "Living in a World of Power and Scarcity."

7

Writing and Evaluating Grant Proposals

INTRODUCTION

If "people give to people," why be concerned about the content of a grant proposal? Because grantmakers must make grants that comply with the tax laws that define their existence. Grantseekers must likewise use grant money for purposes that comply with their tax-exempt purposes. The grant proposal is part of the evidence that grantmakers and grantseekers have complied with the law. Of course, the strongest such evidence will be their annual audits and the programs that their grants achieve.

CONTENT OF PROPOSALS

The grant proposal should communicate to the grantmaker the specific activity to be funded. It should communicate the overall mission of the grantseeker and how the specific activity fits that mission. In my "Successful Fund Raising" class I require that the students prepare a case statement about an agency in the community seeking funding, and also an outline of a full funding proposal. Were I to offer my course to graduate students, I would require them to prepare a complete grant proposal.

The case statement is a public relations statement. It needs to convey the enthusiasm of the grantseeker for the program. It needs to convey the belief that the agency is necessary, even essential, to the community and that the specific program is vital to the agency. Yet the communication cannot seem contrived. Although there may be some general agreement on what is tasteful in a grant proposal, there are bound to be individual differences. Only as the grantseeker learns the personal preferences of the grantmaker can the seeker be more assured that the proposal will communicate the grant information in a way that will motivate the grantmaker to give a gift to the organization.

There are many books and pamphlets in the marketplace about how to write a grant proposal. Basically, though, most of them include the same information. There is probably no right or wrong order to present information; once again, it depends on the preferences of the grantmaker. There is basic information the grantseeker should provide, but the style of the presentation depends on the audience.

The basic information is as follows:

1. The name of the project.

2. The purpose of the project (what community or individuals the project will benefit and how the project will benefit them).

3. How the project will carry out that purpose.

4. Who is responsible for carrying out the project, (list the agency executive director and Board of Directors and their qualifications).

5. How much money and other resources are needed for the project (the budget).

6. How long it will take to complete the project (the time frame).

7. What other sources of funding are available or are being sought and the specific amount requested from this grantmaker.

8. What will happen if the project is not funded.

9. How the project will be evaluated.

10. IRS 501(c)(3) and other verification.

The evaluation of grant requests is the evaluation of each part of the basic information within the framework of the social/political orientation of the grantmaker. Consider the first item, the name of the project. The name or title of the project conveys more than just the type of activity. It conveys the philosophy of the grant-seeker about the activity. For example, I worked with a consortium of church grantmakers, the United Urban Council, in Austin, Texas. One of the projects the council funded was the El Centro de la Gente de Aztlan, a youth center in the barrio of East Austin. The Center was founded by a radical leader in the barrio community who was a member of the "brown berets." The fact that the agency name was in Spanish conveyed the founder's liberal attitude toward bilingualism. A grantmaker would need to be bilingual himself or seek an interpreter just to understand the meaning of the name. The translation of the name is "The Center of the People of Aztlan." The grantmaker would also need to have an understanding of the dynamics of the barrio community to appreciate the significance of the choice of the name, People of Aztlan. Among people with Spanish surnames there are many names they may call themselves, depending on their age, social class, and political orientation, names such as Mexican, Mexican-American, Chicano, Latin-American. Some would consider the name People of Aztlan to be one of the most radical choices of names.

Another example of the significance of name selection is the name for a social work outreach of the Catholic church. I was a maternity caseworker for Catholic Charities in Houston. The agency has also been called Catholic Social Services. The choice of the term *charities* conveys a different social work philosophy than the term *social services*.

The second item of information is the purpose of the project. Once again the social and political philosophies of the grantmaker will affect decisions. In Management by Objectives terminology, the purpose is the "mission," but it may also be the "objective" or "goal" if the project is merely a part of the service of a larger agency or organization. First the grantmaker will evaluate the project within a community context. The exact nature of the community will depend on the focus of the grantmaker: a neighborhood, a city, a state, a region, etc. The grantmaker will consider whether the project duplicates any other service already existing in that community. In other words, is there truly a need for the program? The statement of purpose should articulate the need for the program. Perhaps there are similar programs, but this program is somehow unique. The uniqueness should be stated, but there is a risk of alienating the grantmaker if he is already supporting another existing program. In the case of the El Centro de la Gente de Aztlan, for instance, if the church grantmakers already provided their own outreach to barrio youth, would they be willing to fund a new one?

Another concern for the grantseeker is to beware of jargon in the statement of purpose. The seeker should not approach a corporate grantmaker, for instance, with sociological language that may not be understood. If the grantmaker's language is numbers, or dollars and cents, the grantseeker should use language accordingly.

The third item of information is how the project will carry out its purpose. Here the philosophies of grantmaker and grantseeker are paramount. When I worked for the A.D. Players in Houston, grantmakers who were not allowed to fund religious programs could have easily said no to funding the A.D. Players. To overcome that obstacle, I attempted to argue that all theatre is "religious"; the name *theatre* itself derives from the Greek word theos, meaning god. To participate in my argument, the grantmaker would need to know the reason behind his corporation's or foundation's religious restriction. Perhaps the purpose of the restriction was merely to avoid sectarian grants. In that case a grant to an interdenominational organization like the A.D. Players might be allowed. It is interesting to note how the names of some established organizations have proclaimed a religious purpose, though the stated purpose is less overtly religious, such as the *salvation* in Salvation Army and the C for *Christian* in the YMCA and YWCA.

During the turmoil on college campuses in the late sixties and early seventies, grantmakers became more aware of the need to know how each agency they funded carried out its purpose. Corporate grantmakers found themselves funding universities that hired faculty who had political orientations opposed to corporate philosophies. My own undergraduate alma mater, Stanford University, eventually fired one of my freshman professors, H. Bruce Franklin, who had told us his course would help us to become Marxists. His methods of promoting his philosophy were alien to many Stanford grantmakers.

The answer to the question of how a project carries out its purpose is the most complex part of the grant proposal. It involves the philosophical tension between "effectiveness" and "efficiency" of the agency's work. "Effectiveness" means whether the program fulfills its purpose. "Efficiency" means the ratio of resources to achievements where the resources are financial and affect the allocations of time, materials, personnel, etc. Effectiveness is, of course, more difficult to measure than efficiency. Yet the grantseeker needs to demonstrate to the grantmaker that both effectiveness and efficiency, and the inevitable tension between the two, have been realistically considered. A grantseeker should further explain why a particular resolution of that tension was chosen. For example, if seeking funding for the salary of a master's degree counsellor in a drug treatment agency, the grantseeker needs to explain why a master's degree counsellor, and the higher salary required, is preferable to a bachelor's degree counsellor. Of course, the issue becomes more complicated if the grantseeker is seeking funding for his or her own salary.

At a certain point there will be intangible values that simply cannot be measured. The grantmaker may have to choose between a program that serves adult drug abusers and one that serves teen drug abusers. If possible, the grantmaker may suggest a consolidation of the two programs, but that is not always possible. Or the grantmaker may have to choose between funding new costumes for the opera or new sets for the ballet, or between scholarship programs for two minority groups. Although the grantmaker may claim to be primarily concerned with "prevention," not treatment, or with avoiding being "reactive," or with being on the "cutting edge," personal preferences are nevertheless a real factor. The grantseeker needs to be aware of the grantmaker's preferences and should emphasize how the program fits what the grantmaker wants to do. It will help grantseekers, too, if grantmakers decide their funding priorities and communicate them to the public. There may be some compromise on the part of either the grantmaker or grantseeker, but both parties should avoid compromising so much that they lose sight of their own unique vision.

The fourth item of information is who is responsible for carrying out the project. Legally the Board of Directors is responsible for the activities of the nonprofit agency. The grant proposal should list the names of the Board of Directors and their various titles, for example, John Smith, president, XYZ Corporation. Because "people give to people" it is important for the grantmaker to know who is on the board. Ideally, the board member best acquainted with the grantmaker should present the proposal. Also, many grantmakers require a list of the amounts each board member has already contributed to the project. These grantmakers recognize that a project must have the support of those closest to it in order to encourage others to contribute. Finally, the proposal should also include the resumes of the executive director and staff of the organization or of those who will work directly on the project. It can also include any letters of recommendation or endorsement from community leaders.

The fifth item of information necessary in a grant proposal is how much money and other resources are needed for the project. The budget should be realistic. It should avoid any "miscellaneous" or "other" categories. Many grantseekers will pad their budgets, hoping to get at least a percentage of what they ask. The ethical issue of honesty here is obvious. Another issue is indirect costs such as rent, utilities, or administrative overhead. The Council on Foundations in Washington, D.C., has researched the issue to help both grantmakers and grantseekers. At present there is no uniform method of dealing with such costs, and some grantmakers disallow them altogether. The grantseeker should also identify what in-kind gifts, such as computer time, are needed.

The sixth item of information in the grant proposal is how long it will take to complete the project. The time frame, like the budget, should be realistic. Most grantmakers make annual grants. Will there be a need to renew this grant in future years? Does the project have a measurable completion date? For example, the purposes of some health research programs are accomplished when they find a cure to whatever disease they research. Also, many organizations will need to confront the issue of what they will do when their original founder retires. Does the organization's future depend on just one person? Can there be success without a successor?

The seventh item of information includes what other sources of funding are available or are being sought and the specific amount requested from this grantmaker. It is important for the grantmaker to know what percentage of the total amount has already been contributed and who contributed. It is debatable whether this information should be a total amount or a specific list of each contributor's donations. Some grantmakers may want to know the amount contributed by each person on the Board of Directors, although the total amount given by the board may suffice. The grantmaker will want to be certain that he is not being asked to fund the project alone and will want to know what other sources of support are being considered. Hopefully, the grantmaker will even suggest other sources of funding.

It is usually helpful if the grantmaker is asked for a specific amount of money. Very rarely will a single grantmaker solely fund a project, although some of the larger foundations will sometimes do so. Before requesting a specific amount, the grantseeker should research other grants by the same grantmaker to learn the size of his typical grant. The grantseeker may also ask if the amount being requested is appropriate for that grantmaker.

The eighth item of information is optional. It is the grantseeker's speculation about what will happen if the project is not funded. It is a controversial item because it may be awkward for the grantseeker to admit that the entire organization's future hinges on the next project. On the other hand, it may also be awkward to admit that the organization is merely trying an experimental expansion into the project area and that the organization's commitment to that project area is not yet firmly established. Either way, this information will provide further enlightenment to the grantmaker.

This raises the ethical issue of how much the grantseeker should disclose about the inner workings of the organization. Honesty is the ethical standard. However, it would also be unethical to merely allude to some negative aspect of the organization without giving as complete a picture as possible. It may be that only the chairman of the Board of Directors or the executive director have the most complete picture, and therefore they should be the ones to convey the information. If the grant proposal mentions a controversial or negative aspect of the organization, it should also describe what efforts are being made to remedy the situation. It should never appear that the grantseeker is trying to conceal information.

The ninth item of information is how the project will be evaluated. This item is equally important to grantseekers and grantmakers, but too often both fail to include it. It is important be-

150 Fund Raising, Corporate Giving, Philanthropy

cause it is the information whereby both grantseekers and grantmakers are held accountable for their special tax privileges. There has been criticism of grantmakers in this area. They may make a contribution and never follow up with even a phone call, much less a site visit, to determine if their contribution was used as it was supposed to have been used.

There has been criticism of foundations for not making certain that contributions for research have been used for research. Saul Richman, a former reporter, editor, and public relations director for the Council on Foundations, has suggested that there should be a legal requirement that all research reports sponsored by foundations be made readily available to the public from a central clearinghouse. He cites the case of a midsize foundation that contributed nearly $50,000 to a university professor for historical research. The foundation trustees made the grant because one of the family trustees requested it. The professor never completed the research, but the nonfamily trustees chose to overlook the problem (*Fund Raising Management* 1985:106). A legal mandate to force such research into a public clearinghouse is an extreme solution. What is needed is mutual agreement between the grantmaker and grantseeker about how the grant will be evaluated: who will do the evaluation, how they will do the evaluation, and how much money the evaluation will cost. Evaluation is important to the grantseeker too because it provides a method of quantifying success, to use for credibility for future grants.

The final necessary item of information in a grant proposal is IRS and other verification. The grantseeker should include a copy of the IRS 501(c)(3) form for the organization verifying that it is tax exempt. Grantmakers need this information in order to guarantee that they are meeting IRS requirements for their contributions. Some grantmakers may also request other verification information, such as the organization's most recent audit or a copy of the organization's incorporation verification. The grantseeker should be willing to provide any additional verification information the grantmaker requests.

PACKAGING THE PROPOSAL

The grantseeker will combine all the information into a package that is the grant proposal. Neatness is obviously important, as is careful proofreading, but what sort of "package" is appropriate? The answer depends on the nature of the grantseeking organization and especially the size of its budget. Most grantmakers discourage organizations from spending too large a percentage of their budgets on fund raising. It would be inappropriate to package the grant proposal in a form that includes expensive printing and binding costs.

Grantmakers must be prepared to physically accommodate the grant proposals. Is there adequate filing space? Are all requests retained? Are nonfunded requests disposed of periodically? Is there a record of the status of funding requests from previous years? Eventually the grantmaker will need to computerize all of the pertinent information about the funding requests received. The grantseeker should be certain to routinely provide updated information to the grantmaker too.

The writing of grant proposals and the evaluation of grant proposals are complementary processes. Harmony of the two processes is best achieved when the grantmaker and grantseeker have a satisfactory interpersonal relationship so that either one may freely ask the other for clarification or suggestions. Open communication is part of the concept that "people give to people."

PERSONAL EXPERIENCES

I require the students in my "Successful Fund Raising" class to anonymously critique the case statements and funding proposal outlines of all other students in the class. This exercise allows them to experience part of what the grantmaker experiences in reviewing many funding applications at once. It also allows the students to deal with their defensiveness at having others critique their work. Their final grade is not affected by their classmates' critiques. I read the critiques only after I have given the students my own handwritten evaluation. The exercise does not give a complete view of the "people give to people" dimension, however, because the students address the proposals to corporate or foundation grantmakers. Yet the students' anonymous critiques may be influenced by their interpersonal relationship with the student who wrote the proposal.

It is understandable for grantseekers to be somewhat defensive about their funding proposals. Their ego involvement with the final product is similar to an author with a book. It is important, therefore, for grantmakers to be sensitive to the grantseeker's willingness to accept constructive criticism. Yet, it is also essential that the grantseeker be flexible about changing the proposal in accordance with the grantmaker's recommendation.

Appendix

WOMEN'S FUNDS IN THE UNITED STATES

Federations

Women's Funding Alliance
119 S. Main Street, Suite 330
Seattle, WA 98104
206-467-6733
Dyan Oldenburg, Executive Director
Nine members; founded 1984; 1.5 staff; raised $39,000 in 1985 from payroll deduction pledges; $80,000 from individuals, special events, foundations; allocated $24,000 to members in 1985; holds workshops on racism, heterosexism, managing inherited wealth.

Women's Funding Coalition
817 Broadway, 6th Floor
New York, NY 10003
212-677-1001
Virginia Cornue, Executive Director
Twelve members; staffed; formed 1983; raised $465,000 in 1985 from special events, individuals, corporations, foundations; $11,100 at the workplace; created Committee for Open Workplace Giving—coalition to expand access to New York's public workplace charity drives.

Women's Fund of Greater Washington
1212 Pennsylvania Avenue, S.E.
Washington, DC
202-543-9404
Maia Yaweh, Executive Director
Founded 1984; 15 members; 2 full-time staff; raised $15,000 in 1985; 1986 goal $250,000 from foundations, corporations, special events, individuals (mostly direct mail), some payroll deductions. Not yet making allocations to members; does outreach to women of color groups.

Womens Way
The Sheridan Bldg., 125 S. Ninth Street, #602
Philadelphia, PA 19107
215-592-7212
Lynn Yeakel, Executive Director
Nine members; formed 1976; staff of 5; in 1985 raised about $200,000 from payroll deductions; more than $300,000 from special events, individuals, direct mail, foundations, corporations; allocated $402,000; launched 10th Anniversary Campaign to raise $2 million by 1987.

Public Foundations

Astraea Foundation (local)
P.O. Box 736
New York, NY 10013
212-598-2413
Carol Alpert, Board Member
Incorporated 1976; no staff but plans to hire soon; board 50% women of color; allocates $20,000 to $25,000 each year; raised $50,000 in 1985 from individuals; projects $100,000 this year; endowment long-term goal; focuses on projects that empower women.

Boston Women's Fund (local)
Park Square Building, #902
Boston, MA 02116
617-542-5955
Stefanie Bornes, Program Coordinator
Incorporated 1983; staff of one; raising about $65,000 each year, mostly through special events, some from foundations, direct mail; plans to pursue payroll deductions; offers TA with organizational development, fund raising; funding priorities: low-income women, women of color; will give out $20,000 this year.

Chicago Foundation for Women (local)
332 S. Michigan Avenue, Suite #1419

Chicago, IL 60604
312-922-8762
Pam Anderson, Executive Director
Incorporated 1985 having raised $110,000 from individuals, foundations,
corporations; future plans include direct mail; plans to allocate $100,000
in 1986 to low-income, minority women's groups; trying to raise endowment to cover operating expenses.

Dallas Women's Foundation (local)
9400 N. Central Expressway, #1108
Dallas, TX 75231
214-750-6363
Pat Nicklaus Sabin, Executive Director
Incorporated 1985 having raised $100,000 from 350 individuals; made
grants totaling $25,000; FY 86–87 fund-raising goal—$1 million; will
allocate $50,000, put rest toward $3.5 million endowment; plans TA,
financial education.

Holding Our Own (local)
P.O. Box 3146
Albany, NY 12203
518-436-8111
Carole Friedman, Executive Director
Incorporated 1982; staff of one; with $600,000 endowment, believes
foundation at good size; funds feminist social change, women of color
projects; setting up national revolving loan fund.

Los Angeles Women's Foundation (local)
6030 Wilshire Boulevard, Suite 303
Los Angeles, CA 90036
213-983-9828
Elizabeth Bremner, Project Administrator
Offshoot of S.F. Women's Foundation; incorporated 1985; raised $55,000
from in-kind support, gifts from foundations, corporations, individuals;
1986 goal $150,000, will allocate half; developing funding priorities.

Minnesota Women's Fund (statewide)
Development Office: The Minneapolis Foundation
500 Foshay Tower, 821 Marquette Avenue
Minneapolis, MN 55402
612-339-7374
Karen Frederickson, Development Director
Program Office: 316 University Avenue W.

St. Paul, MN 55103
612-224-6313
Ellen O'Neil, Program Officer
Special Fund of Minneapolis Foundation; set up 1984; 3-year goal to
raise $10 million endowment, $4.6 million collected/pledged so far from
foundations, corporations, individuals, special events; first 2 allocation
cycles 1986.

Ms. Foundation for Women, Inc. (national)
370 Lexington Avenue
New York, NY 10017
212-689-3475
Marie Wilson, Executive Director
Incorporated 1975; 8 staff; raises average of $700,000 each year from
individuals, special events, corporations, foundations, direct mail; building multimillion dollar endowment; gives out about $300,000 each year
to self-help projects working on "survival" issues.

Native Women's Fund of The Seventh Generation Fund (national)
P.O. Box 3505
Reno, NV 89505
702-574-0157
Deborah Harry, Field Representative
Created 1982; staffed; raised $35,000 in 1985 from foundations, individ-
uals (mostly through direct mail); allocated $18,000 in 1985; projects
about same for 1986; funding priorities include locally controlled projects
that promote self-sufficiency, maintenance of traditional ways of life, culture; provides TA, referrals.

Nevada Women's Fund (statewide)
P.O. Box 50428
Reno, NV 89513
702-786-2335
Fritsi H. Erickson, Executive Director
Incorporated 1982; staffed; in 1985 raised $107,000—$60,000 from annual dinner–silent auction, also from corporations, individuals and direct
mail; 1986 goal $125,000; funding priorities include rural areas, elderly,
minorities, displaced homemakers; in 1985 allocated $30,000 in grants;
also awards scholarships—$10,000 in 1985.

The Women's Foundation (local)
3543 18th Street
San Francisco, CA 94110

415-431-1290
Marya Grambs, Co-director
Incorporated 1982; 8 (with exception of Grambs) part-time staff; in 4 years of fund raising has raised $4 million in cash, assets; in 3 years of grantmaking has allocated $400,000 to 100 Bay Area organizations; has raised $500,000 toward endowment.

The Women's Foundation, Orange County (local)
23422 Peralta, Suite I
Laguna Hills, CA 92653
714-855-8187
Betty French Rush, Board Chair
Modeled itself after S.F. Women's Foundation; incorporated 1986; board-run; 1986 fund raising goal $250,000 from foundations, corporations, special events; some to go to endowment; hopes to make first grants late this year; fund raising priorities: low-income women, women of color; planning workshops, seminars.

Foundations Still Forming

Flint Women and Girls Fund (local)
c/o The Flint Public Trust
902–3 Citizens Banking Center–S.
Flint, MI 48502
313-238-5651
Suzanne Feurt, Fund Advisory Council Member
Since 1985 organizing as endowment within local community fund; fund raising goal in neighborhood of $500,000 from special events, direct mail; wants to average $50,000 each year in grants; educating community about needs of women and girls.

The Funds for Women, Inc. (regional)
Heyburn Building, Suite 1215, Broadway at Fourth Avenue
Louisville, KY 40202
502-562-0045
Maxine Brown, Board Member
Incorporated 1985; initiative of Kentucky Foundation for Women; no staff; might get $1 million endowment from sale of stock by major donor, which it hopes to use as challenge to other major donors; development funding priorities.

Funds of the Women's Technical Assistance Project (regional)
1000 Wisconisn Avenue, N.W.
Washington, DC 20007

202-342-2081
Eileen Paul, Director
Unincorporated; 1986 goal to raise developmental funds, largely from religious organizations; plans to support groups that help poor and working poor women in rural areas of Southeast, Southwest.

Michigan Women's Foundation (local)
c/o 526 Allen Street
Lansing, MI 48912
517-372-0160
Ellen Byerlein, Chair, Organizing Committee
Raising money from individuals, special events, and in future, direct mail; unincorporated, unstaffed.

The Sojourner Foundation (local)
Box 182, Ren Cen Station
Detroit, MI 48243
313-568-3800
Sheila Karabees, President
Incorporated 1985; unstaffed; offshoot of Feminist Federal Credit Union; developing fund raising goals, strategies.

Southwest Asdzani Foundation (regional)
c/o Box 4186
Yahtahey, NM 87375
505-722-2144
Gloria Duus, Founding Director
Unincorporated; expects to raise money from foundations, corporations, special events, payroll deductions; future plans include endowment, revolving loan fund, TA; will fund Native American, especially women's, projects stressing self-determination, self-help; setting up board with reps from 4 Southwest tribes.

Women's Community Fund (local)
3130 Mayfield Road, P.O. Box 18129
Cleveland Heights, OH 44118
216-321-3054
Jeanne Van Alta, Board Chair
Incorporated 1983; unstaffed; started off with $40,000 grant from Judy Chicago art project; raised $30,000 in 1985 from special events, individuals, toward goal of $200,000 endowment; projects $40,000 for 1986; will begin grantmaking once reaches endowment.

Women's Source (local)
472 LaFayette Avenue
Westwood, NJ 07675
201-664-3072
Marge Wyngaarden, President
Incorporated 1985; not sure whether it will get off ground; plans unsure.

Private Foundations

Kentucky Foundation for Women (regional)
Heyburn Building, Suite 1215, Broadway at Fourth Avenue
Louisville, KY 40202
502-562-0045
Maxine Brown, Executive Director
Incorporated 1985; staff of one; possible $10 million endowment from
sale of major donor's stock; allocated $60,000 in FY 85, could be up to
$500,000 this year; funding priorities are the arts—believes the arts can
be effective vehicle for social change.

Money for Women's Fund, Inc. (national)
207 Coastal Highway
St. Augustine, FL 32084
904-824-2970
Morgana MacVicar, Coordinator
Incorporated 1976; staffed; raises between $15,000 and $20,000 per year
from individuals; gives average of $10,000 each year to individual fem-
inists in the arts.

Sophia Fund (local)
53 W. Jackson, Rm. 825
Chicago, IL 60604
312-663-1552
Sunny Fischer, Executive Director
Incorporated 1986; all income from one individual; gave out $144,000
in grants in 1985; projects $150,000 this year; funding priorities: repro-
ductive rights, economic justice, prevention of violence against women;
does not fund direct services; some TA and public education.

Wonder Woman Foundation
200 W. Fifty-Seventh Street
New York, NY 10019
(See National Committee for Responsive Philanthropy 1986:8.)

Bibliography

There are hundreds of publications about fund raising and philanthropy. The Foundation Center in New York recently published a bibliography, prepared by Daphne Layton at the American Association of Colleges, containing 1,600 entries, 300 of them annotated.

Universities with philanthropy curricula include City University of New York, Columbia University, Duke Center on Philanthropy, Oral Roberts University, University of Colorado, Yale Program on Non-Profit Organizations (Institute for Social Policy Studies).

The following bibliography provides a personal overview of publications and cited material.

Abundant Life Magazine. "A Pastor Speaks Out On Giving," by Angie Hall, August 1983, p. 20. An interview with a Tulsa pastor.
———. "The Media Have Had Their Say. Now the Truth," by Oral Roberts, September-October 1987, Oral Roberts' response to the media including lifestyle issues.
Adams, Lynda. "The Moral Majority on Capitol Hill." American Association for the Scientific Study of Religion, Southwest, Dallas, 1982. Personal reflections about my own experiences.
———. "Teaching Business Ethics: Problems and Possibilities." American Academy of Religion, Dallas, 1983. Comments regarding my experiences teaching "Successful Fund Raising" at ORU.
———. "Social Work Internships at the U.N." Southwestern Social Sci-

ences Association, San Antonio, 1986. Includes information about my obtaining funding for participation.

American Bible Society. "Printing Press on Target." Newsletter, April 1987. Discussion of the Amity Foundation's work building a printing press in Nanjing, China, with the assistance of the Jiangning Industrial Corporation and local construction workers with the hope of printing Bibles.

Aramony, William. *The United Way*. New York: Donald I. Fine, 1987. The president of United Way summarizes the history and encourages the second-century initiatives of United Way.

Bonjean, Charles M. "Notes for a Workshop at the National Volunteer Conference." Austin, Tex.: Hogg Foundation for Mental Health, June 8, 1986. Mr. Bonjean encouraged me in the publication of this book. His paper describes characteristics of foundations.

Boulding, Kenneth. *The Economics of Love and Fear: A Preface to Grants Economics Analysis*. Belmont, Calif.: Wadsworth, 1973. This is an analysis of the grants economy and the tension between love and fear as motivations for grants.

Broce, Thomas E. *Fund Raising: The Guide to Raising Money From Private Sources*. 2d ed. Norman: University of Oklahoma Press, 1986. (Also available through the Fund Raising Institute.) I use Dr. Broce's text for my "Successful Fund Raising" course, and he has been a guest speaker for the course. His book is also the basic reference for the NSFRE courses. The topics include capital drives, annual support, foundations, corporations, deferred giving, leadership, case statements, proposals, prospect identification and evaluation, and cultivation and solicitation.

CASE. *An Introduction to Fund Raising: The Newcomers' Guide to Development*, edited by Paula J. Faust. Washington, D.C.: Council for Advancement and Support of Education, 1983. A collection of essays from both donors and fund raisers with recommended readings.

———. "Double Your Dollar," 1987. A list of corporations with matching gifts programs for education for 1986–1987.

The Conference Board. *Annual Survey of Corporate Contributions, 1986 Edition: An Analysis of Survey Data for the Calendar Year 1984*, by Linda Cardillo Platzer. New York: The Conference Board, 1986.

Council on Foundations. *Principles and Practices for Effective Grantmaking*. Washington, D.C., 1984. Guidelines for grantmakers.

———. *Alternative Investment Strategies*. Washington, D.C., 1985a. Edited proceedings for a March 1985 conference that includes legal issues and regulatory considerations.

————. *Report on the Philanthropy of Organized Religion*. Washington, D.C., 1985b. A comprehensive report. There is also a report in the September/October 1984 *Foundation News*.

————. *Indirect Costs*. Washington, D.C., 1986a. Research of current policies and practices by grantees and recommendations for grantmakers regarding indirect costs.

————. *Newsletter*. Washington, D.C., July 22, 1986b.

————. *1985 Annual Report*. Washington, D.C., 1986c.

————. *Program-Related Investments: A Primer*. Washington, D.C., 1986d. The primer includes detailed discussion of financial and legal issues as well as case studies. The Piton Foundation staff wrote the primer.

————. *Self-Study Guide for Foundation Boards*. Washington, D.C., 1986e. Sold in sets of ten plus one user guide for either community foundations, private family foundations, or private nonfamily foundations.

————. *1986 Foundation Management Report*. Washington, D.C., 1986f. Bi-annual survey of staff and trustee compensation, employee benefits, and personnel policies. The first survey was in 1984.

————. *1986 Annual Report*. Washington, D.C., 1987.

ECFA. "Application for Membership," 1986.

Edie, John A. *Congress and Foundations: Historical Summary*. Washington, D.C., 1985. A concise history of laws affecting foundations. Mr. Edie is the general counsel of the Council on Foundations.

Flanagan, Joan. *The Successful Volunteer Organization*. Chicago: Contemporary Books, 1981. Detailed information by the author of *The Grass Roots Fundraising Book*, with historical notes about projects by Ben Franklin and Jane Addams, and including discussion of receiving grants from donors whose philosophies differ from the grantseeker's.

Fosdick, Raymond B. *Adventure in Giving*. New York: Harper, 1962. History of the general education board's support of medical schools.

The Foundation Center. *Library Shelf*. An annotated bibliography regularly published by the center describing its recent acquisitions, including articles from *Fund Raising Management*, *Philanthropy Monthly*, *Nonprofit World*, and *Fund Raising Review*.

————. *The National Directory of Corporate Charity*. New York, 1984. Profiles 1,600 U.S. corporations with annual sales of $200 million or more.

————. *Comsearch*. New York, 1986. Printouts by broad topics subjects, geographics, and special topics.

————. *The Foundation Directory*. 11th ed. New York, 1987. Information regarding over 4,400 of the largest U.S. foundations. The *Directory* is considered essential to fund raisers.

————. *National Data Book*. 11th ed. New York, 1987. Information about every active U.S. foundation.

————. *Source Book Profiles 1987*. New York, 1987. Detailed facts about the 1,000 largest U.S. foundations.

Frodsham, Stanley Howard. *Smith Wigglesworth: Apostle of Faith*. Springfield, Mo.: Gospel Publishing House, 1948. Written by Wigglesworth's son-in-law.

Fund Raising Institute. *Monthly Portfolio*. Ambler, Penn. Fund raising ideas and conferences have been published since 1962. The Fund Raising Institute was the first publishing firm to specialize in fund raising publications for nonprofit organizations. It also distributes a free sixteen-page catalog, *Fund Raising Ideas and Techniques*.

————. *Target/1 Fundraiser*. Ambler, Penn., 1986. A computer program to track donors. A demonstration kit is available for $49.50, but the price is refunded if the basic program is purchased within 90 days at a cost of $1,395.

Fund Raising Management. "A Proposal to Make More Studies Available," by Saul Richman, February 1985, p. 106.

————. "Ethical Consideration in Fund Raising," by Douglas E. Freeman, June 1987a, p. 72.

————. "How Key Volunteers Raised $143 Million," by Gary W. Phillips, January 1987b, p. 28.

————. "Involving Key Community Leaders in Your Program," by Jerry A. Linzy, January 1987c, p. 60.

————. "A Question of Generosity," letter to the editor, by Stephen Wertheimer, January 1987d, p. 6.

————. "Charitable Contributions are Likely to Decline," January 1987e, p. 13.

————. July 1987. The entire magazine sue is a special report about religious fund raising, including descriptions of the National Catholic Development Conference and references to Jewish philanthropies, as well as a strong focus on Protestant activities and religious broadcasters.

The Holy Bible, amplified. Grand Rapids: Zondervan Publishing, 1965.

The Holy Bible, New International Version. Grand Rapids: Zondervan Bible Publishers, 1973, 1978.

Houle, Cyril. *The Effective Board*. Battle Creek, Mich.: W. K. Kellogg Foundation, 1960. This early work is cited even today.

Houston Post. "Elite Disburse Foundations' Huge Wealth," by Mary Flood, Olive Talley, and Pete Brewton, July 7, 1985, p. 1A.

Independent Sector. *Professional Forum II Proceedings*. Washington, D.C., 1985. Proceedings from the May 7, 1985, forum, "Governance/ Board Development" and "Attracting and Retaining Talented People in the Field."
———. *1985 Annual Report*. Washington, D.C., 1986.
Internal Revenue Service, Publication 557, *Tax Exempt Status for Your Organization*. Washington, D.C.: 1985.
Knauft, E. B. (Burt). *Profiles of Effective Corporate Giving Programs*. Washington, D.C.: Independent Sector, 1985. This writing summarizes the research of Mr. Knauft, the former vice president of corporate social responsibility and former vice president and executive director of Aetna Life and Casualty and its corporate foundation, written while he was a Visiting Fellow at the Program on Non-Profit Organizations at Yale University. He is currently executive vice president of Independent Sector.
Levitt, Zola. Newsletter. Dallas, June 1, 1987.
Lohmann, Roger A. *Breaking Even: Financial Management in Human Service Organizations*. Philadelphia: Temple University Press, 1980. One section is devoted to fund raising and includes a description of management of collections recommended by the American Institute for Certified Public Accountants.
Menninger, Roy W. *Foundation Work May be Hazardous to Your Mental Health: Some Occupational Dangers of Grantmaking and Grantreceiving*. Washington, D.C.: Council on Foundations, 1981. Dr. Menninger suggests that narcissism, guilt, and gratitude are motivations for giving. He explores psychological aspects of giving and receiving grants, urging both parties to work toward mutual respect and appreciation rather than power and dependency.
Ministries Today. "America: Nation of Givers," by Jamie Buckingham, September/October 1986a, p. 21. The author challenges the figures in the Council on Foundations' religion study because he claims it lumps earned income, such as what CBN receives for cable and satellite hookups and what Oral Roberts receives from ORU, with contributions.
———. "Church Audits Under the Tax Reform Act," by James Guinn, September/October 1986b, p. 16.
National Committee for Responsive Philanthropy. *Responsive Philanthropy*, Winter 1980.
———. *Responsive Philanthropy*, Spring 1986.
———. *1986 Annual Report*. Washington, D.C., 1987a.
———. *Responsive Philanthropy*, Winter 1987b.
National Society of Fund Raising Executives. Membership brochure.

Nielsen, Waldemar. *The Big Foundations.* New York: Columbia University Press, 1972.

———. *The Goldon Donors.* New York: E. P. Dutton, 1985. This is an update of *The Big Foundations* with entertaining descriptions of the largest U.S. foundations and the social and political factors that influence them.

The Nonprofit Times. "Study Details Rise in New Foundations," by Larry Blumenthal, December 1987, p. 3.

O'Connell, Brian. *The Board Member's Book.* New York: The Foundation Center, 1985. Mr. O'Connell is the founding president of Independent Sector. His vast experience in volunteerism includes work with the American Heart Association and, as national director, with the Mental Health Association.

Odendah, Teresa J., ed. *America's Wealthy and the Future of Foundations.* New York: The Foundation Center, 1987. These readings, cosponsored by the Council on Foundations and Yale Program on Non-Profit Organizations, examine trends in the formation of foundations.

Odendah, Teresa Jean, Elizabeth Trocolli Boris, and Arlene Kaplan Daniels. *Working in Foundations: Career Patterns of Women and Men.* New York: The Foundation Center, 1985. This study provides insights for those currently employed in foundations and for those seeking such employment. Dr. Odendah, an anthropologist, is executive director of the Women's Foundation of Colorado in Denver, and Dr. Boris is vice president for research and planning at the Council on Foundations.

Payton, Robert. "Major Challenges to Philanthropy." Washington, D.C.: Independent Sector, 1984. Mr. Payton, president of Exxon Education Foundation, presented this discussion paper at the Independent Sector Annual Meeting. Chapters include philanthropy as a vocation and the philanthropic tradition. He considers classic writings such as Saint Thomas Aquinas. He also suggests other sources such as Robert Bremner's *American Philanthropy*, David Rothman's *Doing Good*, and James Douglas' *Why Charity*.

Pennzoil Perspectives. "National Merit Scholars Honored," by Lynda Adams, 1979, p. 14.

———. "Pennzoil Joins March of Dimes, Superwalk," May 1980, p. 3.

Reagan, Ronald. "Remarks by the President at Briefing for National Philanthropy Day." The White House, November 14, 1986.

Ross, R. J. *Fund Raising for New Agencies.* Elkhart, Ind.: Samaritan Institute, 1978. I also use this booklet in my course at ORU.

Seymour, Harold J. (Si). *Designs for Fund Raising: Principles, Patterns,*

Techniques. New York: McGraw-Hill Book Co., 1966. This book is still quoted today. For example, on the topic of donor cultivation: "You can't make a good pickle just by squirting vinegar on a cucumber—it has to soak awhile." It is also available through the Fund Raising Institute.

Stanford Observer. "John Gardner, Citizen: Individual Gifts Provide Bulk of Non-Profit Groups' Support," by Donald Stokes, October 1983.

———. "How Stanford Manages Its Endowment," by Julia Sommer, October 1986a.

———. "Gifts that Provide Income to the Givers," by Julia Sommer, November 1986b.

The Support Center. *The Support Center News.* Oklahoma City, 1986.

Swan, Sandra S. Telephone interview of New York Junior League president, by the author, October 8, 1987.

United Way. "United Way Policy Against Coercion," United Way Public Relations Department, July 1987, p. 2.

Van Bijlert, Jan. *Inmates of St. Job's Hospital, Utrecht, Soliciting Donations.* Painting, 1630s. This is the only known Dutch group portrait of poor people. The artist, a member of the hospital's board, painted this in response to the township's attempt to revoke the hospital's right to hold annual charitable drives. In the sixteenth century, Dutch reformers during Protestant-Catholic struggles accused the church of spending too much on art and giving too little to the poor.

Waldo, Charles N. *Boards of Directors.* Westport, Conn.: Greenwood Press, 1985. Includes a comparison of nonprofit and profit boards.

White, Arthur A. *The Charitable Behavior of Americans: Findings from a National Survey.* Washington, D.C.: Independent Sector, 1986. Yankelovich, Skelly and White, Inc., conducted this study commissioned by the Rockefeller Brothers Fund.

White, Benjamin T. *A Primer on the Tax Consequences of Corporate Giving.* Washington, D.C.: Council on Foundations, 1987. A comprehensive discussion of corporate contributions including the effects of the 1986 Tax Reform Act.

Index

About the Author

LYNDA LEE ADAMS-CHAU teaches "Successful Fund Raising" at Oral Roberts University. She is a practicing attorney in Oklahoma.